LUKE: A Daily Dialogue with God

3 months with the Life of Christ

**written & edited by
Gladys Hunt**

Best wishes! Gladys Hunt

with Reflections from Scripture Union

Harold Shaw Publishers
Wheaton, Illinois

Copyright © 1986 by Gladys Hunt & Scripture Union

All rights reserved. No part of this book may be reproduced or transmitted in any form or by any means, electronic or mechanical, including photocopying, recording, or any information storage and retrieval system without written permission from Harold Shaw Publishers, Box 567, Wheaton, Illinois 60189. Printed in the United States of America.

"Reflections" are based on notes by Scripture Union authors and are used by permission of Scripture Union, 7000 Ludlow St., Upper Darby, PA 19082.

Cover photo: John Shaw

ISBN 0-87788-510-9

96 95 94 93 92 91 90 89 88 87 86

10 9 8 7 6 5 4 3 2 1

Contents

Introduction to Luke's Gospel 5

How to Use This Book 7

1 **Birth and Childhood Narratives** 10
   1:1–2:52 *(8 studies)*

2 **Preparation for the Good News** 28
   3:1–4:13 *(3 studies)*

3 **Jesus in Galilee** 36
   4:14–9:45 *(20 studies)*

4 **Traveling toward Jerusalem** 78
   9:46–19:27 *(28 studies)*

5 **Jesus in Jerusalem** 136
   19:28–21:38 *(6 studies)*

6 **Jesus' Last Hours with His Disciples** 150
   22:1–53 *(3 studies)*

7 **The Arrest and Crucifixion** 158
   22:54–23:56 *(4 studies)*

8 **The Resurrection** 168
   24:1–53 *(3 studies)*

   Prayer Notebook 176

   God Is Speaking to Me About . . . 178

   Key Verses 180

Introduction to Luke's Gospel

Luke has the distinction of being the only non-Jewish New Testament writer. He was a doctor by profession (Col. 4:14), which may account for his love of detail and the compassion with which he recounts events in Jesus' ministry. His book is the longest of the four gospels and the most beautifully written.

This gospel was the first of two documents Luke addressed to a man named Theophilus. The second was *The Acts of the Apostles* (see Acts 1:1). The salutation, "most excellent Theophilus," may indicate that he was a high official. Luke may have been writing to an earnest inquirer, and he was diligent to give as complete a picture of Jesus as he could.

Luke was a careful scholar and his Greek was notably good. As a close friend of Paul's, he undoubtedly knew many of the apostles who could help him in his research. He was with Paul for two years during Paul's imprisonment in Caesarea. During that time he had opportunity to interview the people who knew Jesus best. The detailed information he shares about the births of John the Baptist and Jesus may very well have come from long talks with Mary, the mother of Jesus.

Notice, too, the careful way Luke dates the events in this book. When he writes of the emergence of John the Baptist, for example, he gives six contemporary datings by which to pin-point the time when "the word of God came to John" (3:1–2).

The *lordship* of Christ is emphasized throughout Luke's writing. Jesus insists on a radical kind of discipleship, and he speaks of disciples who "daily take up their cross," renounce all, and follow hard after him.

Luke highlights God's concern for the poor and the disenfranchised. The story of the rich man and Lazarus appears in his gospel alone. Luke shows our Lord ministering to Gentiles, calling sinners to himself, and giving women honor and encouragement. He is sensitive to all segments of society not represented in the basic power structure of that day.

Luke details Jesus' prayer life, particularly at his life's great crisis points. He also includes the praise hymns of Zechariah and Mary. The love of God shines out in this narrative of Jesus' life and death. Only Luke gives us the stories Jesus told about how much God loves the lost (Luke 15).

Luke may not have been an eyewitness to the life of Jesus on earth, but we are greatly indebted to him for his painstaking and accurate work as a historian. His book makes wonderful reading and points to an even more wonderful Savior.

☐ Outline of the Gospel of Luke

I. Birth and Childhood Narratives   *1:1–2:52*
  A. John's birth and mission foretold   *1:1–25*
  B. Jesus' birth and mission foretold   *1:26–56*
  C. Zechariah's blessing   *1:57–80*
  D. Jesus' birth   *2:1–40*
  E. The boy Jesus at the temple   *2:41–52*

II. Preparation for the Good News   *3:1–4:13*
  A. John the Baptist's ministry   *3:1–14*
  B. Jesus' baptism   *3:15–23*
  C. Jesus' temptation   *4:1–13*

III. Jesus in Galilee   *4:14–9:45*
  A. Jesus in Nazareth and Capernaum   *4:14–44*
  B. Jesus' call to faith   *5:1–6:11*
  C. Jesus' call and teaching of the Twelve   *6:12–49*
  D. Jesus' compassion   *7:1–50*
  E. Understanding Jesus' ministry   *8:1–56*
  F. Understanding who Jesus is   *9:1–45*

IV. Traveling toward Jerusalem   *9:46–19:27*
  A. Realities of discipleship   *9:46–10:42*
  B. Teaching about prayer   *11:1–13*
  C. Jesus' response to criticism   *11:14–12:12*
  D. Jesus' instructions to his disciples   *12:13–12:59*
  E. Call to repentance and faith   *13:1–35*
  F. Teaching about values   *14:1–16:31*
  G. Forgiveness and faith   *17:1–19*
  H. The coming kingdom   *17:20–18:30*
  I. Jesus nearing Jerusalem   *18:31–19:27*

V. Jesus in Jerusalem   *19:28–21:38*
  A. Triumphal entry   *19:28–48*
  B. Teaching in the temple area   *20:1–21:4*
  C. Signs of the end of the age   *21:5–38*

VI. Jesus' Last Hours with His Disciples   *22:1–53*
  A. The upper room   *22:1–38*
  B. In the garden   *22:39–53*

VII. Arrest and Crucifixion   *22:54–23:56*
  A. Denial and mockery   *22:54–71*
  B. Trial   *23:1–25*
  C. Crucifixion and burial   *23:26–56*

VIII. Resurrection   *24:1–53*
  A. Empty tomb   *24:1–12*
  B. Road to Emmaus   *24:13–35*
  C. Joyful disciples   *24:36–53*

How to Use This Book

What you are about to do in the following pages is not just study the Bible. That's only part of it. You see, God speaks directly to you through the words of the Bible. And in prayer, you can speak to him. As you learn to perform these two activities together you'll discover a dynamic, two-way communication with God.

Each two-page daily study is built around a simple yet profound four-step plan: *Pray, Read, Meditate, Pray.*

☐ PRAY

Ask the Holy Spirit to help you understand and apply what you are about to read. You may pray the written prayer or simply use it as a guide to your own prayer. Ask for a sharp mind and an open, honest heart. Remember, God *wants* to speak to you through his Word.

☐ READ

When you read the passage for the day, read it slowly and deeply. Resist the temptation to think, "Oh, I know what these verses say because I've read them so many times." Try reading the passage several times to make sure you get it all. Don't expect to hear God's still small voice if you whisk through the verses in a few seconds.

☐ MEDITATE

Don't be scared off by the word *meditate*. It definitely does not mean Eastern meditation where the goal is simply to empty yourself. Rather, Christian meditation consists of pushing away your day-to-day thoughts and worries in order to fill yourself with thoughts of God and his Word. This studyguide will help you meditate on God's Word with the following features:

Discovery. Use your God-given intellect and carefully answer the four questions for each day, referring to the excerpts from commentaries when you need to. But don't parrot the answers you've heard others give or that you think are correct or that sound good. Find your own answers. What does the text actually say? What does it mean? What does it mean to you? How does it apply to your life?

Reflection. After working through the passage on your own, read the comments on the verses. See if your personal discoveries are confirmed or if your hanging questions are answered. Also, see if the Reflection touches on something you've overlooked or gives you a new insight.

My Response. Next, you come to an important feature: your response to what you have learned. Here you have an opportunity to express whatever is on your heart and mind. You may want to write out your praise and thanks to God based on what you have read or you may want to respond to God's Word by writing down a specific way you plan to apply what you've learned. Or you may simply want to crystalize what you feel is the most memorable truth of the day's passage. But after listening to God speak to you through reading the Scriptures, answering questions and reading the Reflection, you need to begin *your* part of the "conversation."

Memory Point. To reinforce the theme of each chapter, a Key Verse has been selected. The Memory Point for each day gives you a short suggestion to help you memorize or review the verse. God's Word, committed to instant recall, can straighten your mental perspective, meet your emotional needs, and repel the Enemy's attacks. The eight Key Verses are printed on the last two pages of this book. Each is printed from the NIV, and there is also a space for you to write in another translation of each verse, if you prefer. You'll want to refer back to this page often since memorization requires regular review.

☐ PRAY

Finally, pray again for help in applying God's Word. If you truly believe the Bible is God's Word and that God does speak to you in it, then you must respond. And that's not always easy, but God will give you the ability and even the desire to do what he wants if you ask him. The prayer suggestions will help you get started, but don't stop there! Your prayer can and should also proceed to confession, thanksgiving or praise, and intercession.

☐ Bonus Features

At the back of the book you will find two additional features that will enhance your walk with God and help you keep a record of what he is doing in your life.

Prayer Notebook. Some Christians think, "I know God answers prayer, but I don't often see it." The problem most of us have is that God answers many of our prayers, but we simply forget! By keeping track of your prayer life you will see how God *is* answering your prayers. When you have a request you want to bring to the Lord, jot it down in your Prayer Notebook along with the date. Then begin praying about it. When God answers, according to his own time schedule, record the date you receive the answer.

God Is Speaking To Me About . . . This is your opportunity to record major spiritual breakthroughs as well as key actions you are prompted to take whose date you want to recall. For example, you may sense God's direction to reach out to a certain neighbor, or you may receive a new insight into the meaning of your relationship with God. Record these insights in this special section you'll find at the back of this book.

☐ Tips for Daily Bible Study

Daily Bible study and prayer are essential if you are to grow to be a stronger, more joyful Christian. Here are six tips that will help you:

1. *Make a commitment.* Put your decision to have daily Bible study and prayer in writing, on a 3x5 card or at the front of this book. Tell your spouse or close friend of your commitment and ask him or her to check up on you occasionally. Finally, tell God of your commitment and ask for his help in sticking to it.

2. *Use a Bible that is clear to you.* Since so many good translations are available today, find one that you enjoy and trust. Occasionally try a new version for familiar passages. Of course you cannot use this book without your Bible.

All quotes are from the *New International Version* unless otherwise noted. However, special care has been taken to make this studyguide usable with any Bible version, traditional or contemporary.

3. *Establish a routine.* Plan to study God's Word at the same time each day. Find a spot where you can be alone. Keep your Bible, this book, and a pen together in one place so you don't have to hunt for them. Daily Bible study becomes easier when it's part of your daily schedule.

4. *Don't let guilt impede your progress.* There will be days when you can't keep up your normal schedule. Don't listen to Satan's accusations at times like that; simply pick up where you left off.

5. *Expect to meet God.* The purpose for daily Bible study is not to become a Bible know-it-all or to prove that you are a super-Christian or to fulfill some obligation. Knowing God better and growing in your relationship should be your goal.

6. *Plan to keep going.* Don't let the end of this book be the end of a daily time for reading, meditation, and prayer. Get another studyguide or set up your own study schedule. As you soak in God's Word daily your life becomes fertile soil which God can use to create beautiful new growth.

☐ Have a Good Time

Finally, enjoy this! Too many Christians think of daily Bible study as drudgery. That's just the lie that Satan wants you to believe. You may have to work at sticking to your commitment, but if you stick with it, you'll find your daily appointment with God is the most rewarding part of your Christian life. Nothing is more exciting than hearing God speak directly to you through his Word, and enjoying the privilege of two-way communication with your Creator and Lord.

1/Birth and Childhood Narratives
Luke 1:1–2:52

☐ Introduction

Imagine that you are Dr. Luke, a Greek physician, researching the details of the life of Jesus Christ.

You have heard Paul preach convincingly about who Jesus is and about a salvation that comes only through believing in him as the Son of God. Convicted by the Holy Spirit that Paul speaks the truth, you have become a Christian. Your commitment to Jesus grows as you travel with Paul and hear him teach the great truths about God's redemptive plan.

Now, at the encouragement of Theophilus, your opportunity has come to write the story of Jesus. You want to go back to the beginning. How did Jesus come to earth? What were the details of his coming? Who was involved in the preparation for his Advent?

You have stayed with Paul during his imprisonment in Caesarea, and now you have located Mary, the mother of Jesus, and been introduced to her through the apostles.

Think of all the questions you might ask her. Picture Luke listening intently as Mary shares this awesome story. How would he determine what to include in his retelling of these sacred events?

It is evident that the Holy Spirit carefully guided Luke in what he wrote down for us to read so long after his time. Luke wonderfully recorded what is relevant to the full purpose of Jesus' life and death. The other details which might cause us to be sidetracked are not told. Jesus came as the Savior. That is what is important. And the way was prepared for him by John the Baptist. We hear only enough of John's story to understand how God fulfilled all that he promised in the Old Testament when he said a messenger would come to call out, "Prepare the way for the Lord."

As you read the incredible details of John's birth and his father Zechariah's wonderful song of praise, imagine that you are Luke hearing this for the first time and recording it in your heart and mind. Then, when you hear Mary tell of the angel coming to her, of the actual birth of Jesus, and of all the wondrous events that surrounded it, you will want to retain in your heart and mind the Key Verse chosen for this section of our study. Make it part of the truth you live by.

☐ Key Verse 1: Luke 1:37
For nothing is impossible with God.

☐ Outline of the Gospel of Luke

I. Birth and Childhood Narratives 1:1–2:52
   A. John's birth and mission foretold 1:1–25
   B. Jesus' birth and mission foretold 1:26–56
   C. Zechariah's blessing 1:57–80
   D. Jesus' birth 2:1–40
   E. The boy Jesus at the temple 2:41–52

II. Preparation for the Good News 3:1–4:13
   A. John the Baptist's ministry 3:1–14
   B. Jesus' baptism 3:15–23
   C. Jesus' temptation 4:1–13

III. Jesus in Galilee 4:14–9:45
   A. Jesus in Nazareth and Capernaum 4:14–44
   B. Jesus' call to faith 5:1–6:11
   C. Jesus' call and teaching of the Twelve 6:12–49
   D. Jesus' compassion 7:1–50
   E. Understanding Jesus' ministry 8:1–56
   F. Understanding who Jesus is 9:1–45

IV. Traveling toward Jerusalem 9:46–19:27
   A. Realities of discipleship 9:46–10:42
   B. Teaching about prayer 11:1–13
   C. Jesus' response to criticism 11:14–12:12
   D. Jesus' instructions to his disciples 12:13–12:59
   E. Call to repentance and faith 13:1–35
   F. Teaching about values 14:1–16:31
   G. Forgiveness and faith 17:1–19
   H. The coming kingdom 17:20–18:30
   I. Jesus nearing Jerusalem 18:31–19:27

V. Jesus in Jerusalem 19:28–21:38
   A. Triumphal entry 19:28–48
   B. Teaching in the temple area 20:1–21:4
   C. Signs of the end of the age 21:5–38

VI. Jesus' Last Hours with His Disciples 22:1–53
   A. The upper room 22:1–38
   B. In the garden 22:39–53

VII. Arrest and Crucifixion 22:54–23:56
   A. Denial and mockery 22:54–71
   B. Trial 23:1–25
   C. Crucifixion and burial 23:26–56

VIII. Resurrection 24:1–53
   A. Empty tomb 24:1–12
   B. Road to Emmaus 24:13–35
   C. Joyful disciples 24:36–53

1

☐ **PRAY for insight into God's Word**
Lord, thank you for Luke's faithfulness in writing this book. Now help me, by your grace, to be faithful in studying it, for Jesus' sake.

☐ **READ Luke 1:1–13**

☐ **MEDITATE on God's Word**

Discovery
1. Why did Luke write this Gospel? What were his sources of information according to verses 2 and 3? Compare verses 1–4 with Acts 1:1–2.

2. Who were Elizabeth and Zechariah? Note at least five facts that help you know them.

3. How might the fact that Roman soldiers occupied their nation have affected the prayers of Zechariah and the people (10)? What might they have been praying about?

4. Why do you think God sent an angel to Zechariah instead of simply letting the events take place? List the ways in which the angel was both personal and specific in what he said. What does this tell you about God and his relationship with you?

Birth and Childhood Narratives/Luke 1:1–2:52

Reflection

Luke was concerned about helping his prominent friend Theophilus understand about Jesus Christ. He wanted to show him that the truths of the gospel are firmly and reliably anchored in history. The Holy Spirit used Luke's concern for his friend to inspire the writing of this gospel. He begins with the story of Zechariah and Elizabeth.

A righteousness that counts (5–7). Notice the important words, "upright in the sight of God." Zechariah was a priest of the division of Abijah. (The cycle of priestly duties was divided into twenty-four divisions; priests served one week at a time, twice a year.) Elizabeth herself was a priest's daughter (5). The distinctive feature of this couple's profession of godliness, however, was that it was not only outwardly correct but inwardly real—a reality demonstrated by its power to sustain disappointment, for Elizabeth was barren.

A prayer that was heard (8–13). This prayer was more probably offered for the redemption of Israel than for the gift of a son. Zechariah illustrates the truth that "the prayer of a righteous man is powerful and effective" (James 5:16). God answered by promising a son who was to be the forerunner of the Redeemer—something far beyond Zechariah's appeal.

My Response

Memory Point

Copy Key Verse 1 on a 3x5 card and place it where you can review it often. "Nothing is impossible with God" (Luke 1:37).

☐ **PRAY to apply God's Word**

Ask God to help you understand what it means to be upright in the sight of God and to point out areas in your life that are inconsistent with this goal . . .

2

☐ **PRAY for insight into God's Word**
Father, I need to learn new things about your faithfulness. Teach me today, I pray, in Jesus' name.

☐ **READ Luke 1:14–25**

☐ **MEDITATE on God's Word**

Discovery
1. What remarkable things did the angel tell Zechariah about the son he would have? Make a list.

2. What part would this child play in the redemption of the Jewish people?

3. How did Zechariah respond to this news from the angel? Why? Why are we often slow to believe that God means what he says, even when we have strong evidence of truth?

4. What further sign did Zechariah receive from the Lord that what the angel predicted was true? How did God show his faithfulness to Zechariah and Elizabeth?

Reflection

Everything about this story of two ordinary people is remarkable because God had a plan in mind.

Remarkable promises. John's greatness was to be the kind that really matters— "in the sight of the Lord" (15). He was to be uniquely gifted with the Holy Spirit. Earlier prophets had known this gift for limited periods of prophetic activity, but John had it continuously from birth, thus guaranteeing his success in making ready a people for the coming of the Messiah (17).

Remarkable unbelief. Zechariah asked for a sign (18), in view of the human impossibility of what was promised. The sign he received was a rebuke to his unbelief. His unbelief was surprising since he himself had prayed for God to do something for the redemption of Israel and to grant him and his wife a son (13). Zechariah and Elizabeth both believed in God's power, aware of what he had done for a woman like Sarah. Furthermore, God actually sent the angel Gabriel to give added assurance about what was to happen (19).

Remarkable faithfulness on God's part. How long do you think Zechariah and Elizabeth had been praying for a child? Childlessness was considered a reproach from God in those days (25). Probably by this time they no longer prayed for a child but concentrated their prayers on the deliverance of Israel and the Messiah who was to come. Faithfully, and beyond their expectation, God answered both prayers.

My Response

Memory Point

Repeat Key Verse 1 (Luke 1:37) aloud and think of how appropriate this truth was in the life of Elizabeth and Zechariah.

☐ **PRAY to apply God's Word**

Thank you, God, that you don't alter your faithfulness toward me, even when I respond in unbelief. Make me aware today of all the ways you show your faithfulness to me . . .

3

☐ **PRAY for insight into God's Word**
Lord, help me to put aside all the thoughts that distract my attention from your Word. Let me hear you say something for my life today.

☐ **READ Luke 1:26–38**

☐ **MEDITATE on God's Word**

Discovery
1. Note the precision of details that answer the questions *who, what, when,* and *where* in verses 26–27. What did the angel tell Mary about herself? About the child she was to bear?

2. Who would be the parents of this child? Notice the angel's careful explanation of how Mary would become pregnant (35). What names were given to this child in verses 31, 32, and 35?

3. What was significant about Mary's response to the angel? How did this differ from Zechariah's response (1:18, 20)?

4. Why do you think the angel told Mary the news about Elizabeth's pregnancy (36)? What truth about God did the angel want to emphasize? Can you accept God's promises for your life with Mary's kind of faith, confident that the angel's words in verse 37 are true?

Reflection

In today's reading, the second part of God's plan is initiated. Notice how carefully he takes care of the details.

God's choice. Sovereign as that choice was, everything that we learn of Mary underlines how suitable she was for her God-given task. Mary did not doubt what the angel said; rather, she asked how such a miracle as virgin conception could take place (34). Her response to the remarkable answer is an example of submissive obedience to the word of God (38).

God's Son. While "Jesus" was to be his human name (31), all the descriptive titles given to him left Mary in no doubt as to his deity (32–33). Indeed it would be appropriate for the wise men to seek him out as the King, for the Old Testament prophecies, promised to the Messiah of Davidic lineage, were fulfilled in Christ (2 Sam. 7:13; Ps. 89:26–29).

God's power. The answer to Mary's question, "How?" was a statement concerning the Holy Spirit (35), for it is he who carries out all of God's purposes. He was to equip the Messiah for his ministry (Luke 4:18); and, after his death, he was to raise him to life again (Rom. 1:4). He would then become the chief witness to humanity of this same Jesus as the Savior (John 16:12–15).

My Response

Memory Point

Do you believe that nothing is impossible with God? Encourage a friend with this Key Verse today.

☐ PRAY to apply God's Word

Father, help me to be more like Mary, quick to say *your will be done* rather than *my will be done*. Thank you that nothing is impossible with you . . .

4

☐ **PRAY for insight into God's Word**
Dear Lord, teach me today how to praise you; remind me again who you are.

☐ **READ Luke 1:39–56**

☐ **MEDITATE on God's Word**

Discovery
1. How do you explain Elizabeth's joy and insight at the arrival of Mary? What three blessings did she give?

2. How did Elizabeth describe the child Mary would bear?

3. In Mary's response, called the Magnificat, what did she say about her relationship with God?

4. What did Mary tell about God's character in verses 46–55? Compare Mary's words with Hannah's prayer in 1 Samuel 2:1–10.

Reflection

Mary probably needed to talk over what had happened to her with someone she trusted, and so she set off to visit her relative, Elizabeth. Imagine Mary's delight when Elizabeth, by the Spirit's revelation, already understood what had happened.

A spiritual recognition (39–45). As soon as Mary greeted Elizabeth, Elizabeth felt a remarkable movement in her womb (41)—it was a leap for joy (44)! To confirm this fact, Elizabeth experienced the infilling of the Holy Spirit so that she might rightly interpret this event. She plainly identified Mary's unborn baby as her Lord, the Messiah (43).

A spiritual example (46–56). Mary's response was to worship God. Mary's praise was the expression of deeply felt convictions. Her words are remarkable for their reference to so many attributes of God: his saving power (47), his condescension (48), his might (49), his holiness (49), his sovereignty (51–52), his compassion (53), his willingness to help his people (54), his mercy (54), and his faithfulness (55). Her song of praise is full of Old Testament allusions, not because she had the Old Testament open before her as we may have, but because it had become part of her whole outlook.

My Response

Memory Point

Both Mary and Elizabeth experienced the truth of Key Verse 1. Do you believe it as you repeat it? "Nothing is impossible with God" (Luke 1:37).

☐ PRAY to apply God's Word

Lord, give me the same kind of confidence Mary experienced to know that you are working out your will through my life. Give me humility and submission to your sovereignty . . .

5

☐ **PRAY for insight into God's Word**
Lord, already this day has been full of your mercies. As I study today, help me to recognize your faithfulness to your people throughout history.

☐ **READ Luke 1:57–80**

☐ **MEDITATE on God's Word**

Discovery
1. What was the response of the neighbors and relatives at the birth of John (57–66)? What conclusion did they reach about this child?

2. When Zechariah began to speak again, he indicated that John's birth was a sign of God acting on behalf of his people. Make a list of what God was doing in verses 68–75.

3. For what purpose was God saving his people (74–75)? Apply this to your own life.

4. What did Zechariah prophesy about the role John would play in the salvation of the people (76–80)?

Reflection

The name John means "God is gracious"—gracious in giving a son to this couple after many years of prayerful waiting; gracious in giving his people a prophet after a gap of several hundred years. This prophet would prepare the way for the one who would be "full of grace and truth" (John 1:14).

God's mercy lifted up in praise (67–79). A horn is a symbol of strength in an animal, and "a horn of salvation" means a *powerful* salvation (69). "The tender mercy of our God" is a key phrase (78). Mercy is warm affection demonstrated to those who are needy, helpless, and distressed. There was a real danger that the people of John's day would not recognize the Messiah since they often interpreted God's promises in a political and material way rather than a spiritual way. God used John to help them return to a spiritual understanding so that they would be ready for the Messiah.

God's mercy in human experience. As Christians we may rejoice that Christ has conquered all our enemies (71), lightened our darkness (78–79), removed the shadow of death (79), found us and brought us back to God (79). We are, however, not without obligations—we are saved to *serve* and to *live holy and righteous lives* (74–75).

My Response

Memory Point

Meditate today on the implications of Key Verse 1 (Luke 1:37) in your own life, the life of your family, and in your business affairs. Repeat the verse from memory.

☐ PRAY to apply God's Word

Thank you, heavenly Father, for your great mercy in remembering us and keeping your promises. Help me to live today trusting in your faithfulness . . .

6

☐ **PRAY for insight into God's Word**
Lord, as I study today, make me more aware of what your birth as a human being means for me and for the world.

☐ **READ Luke 2:1–20**

☐ **MEDITATE on God's Word**

Discovery
1. From a human point of view, how did Jesus happen to be born in Bethlehem? From God's point of view, why was he born in Bethlehem? (See Micah 5:2 for the Old Testament prophecy.)

2. Describe the contrast between the simplicity of Jesus' birth and the grandeur of his birth announcement. Why were the angels so full of joy and praise to God?

3. Trace the progression of the shepherds' emotions in verses 8–20.

4. Use your imagination to describe what may have been Mary's thoughts throughout her pregnancy, the trip to Bethlehem, and the birth of her special baby. How did God use the shepherds to confirm the faith she evidenced in Luke 1:38?

Reflection

Caesar Augustus decreed a census for his own purposes. But the sovereign purpose of God was fulfilled in that decree (Gal. 4:4). God's *sovereignty* and *faithfulness* go together, for in the birth of God's Son in Bethlehem, an Old Testament prophecy was fulfilled (Matt. 2:4–6). Even more amazing was the truth of God's *condescension:* his Son was born of a woman, laid in a manger, made poor for our sakes (2 Cor. 8:9).

The first announcement was made by angels to shepherds. The dignity of the messengers underlined the importance of the message—its origins were in heaven. Shepherds had something of a bad reputation and were a despised class of men. But they were the first to hear—the coming of the Savior is Good News for all people.

Their first reaction was fear (9). They had never before seen such glory. But one of the major purposes of Jesus' birth was the removal of fear, and the angel's first words were, "Do not be afraid" (10).

The shepherds became *the first visitors* (15–16). The right response to any revelation from God is to investigate and ponder it. In their own way, the shepherds did what Mary did (19).

Not surprisingly, the shepherds became *the first preachers* of the Christmas message (17–20). The message was for all (10), so they proclaimed it to all they knew (17–18).

My Response

Memory Point

The angels knew that "Nothing is impossible with God." The shepherds experienced what they thought was impossible. Can you believe this verse for the ordinary things of life as well?

☐ PRAY to apply God's Word

Lord, let me be like Mary and ponder your words. Let me also be like the shepherds who shared them with others . . .

7

☐ **PRAY for insight into God's Word**
Dear God, as I study today help me to see your faithfulness in keeping your promises.

☐ **READ Luke 2:21–40**

☐ **MEDITATE on God's Word**

Discovery
1. Notice how carefully Mary and Joseph kept the Jewish law in regard to Jesus' birth. What four actions did they take (21–22, 24)? Why was he given the name *Jesus* (1:31)?

2. Using your own words, describe Simeon. What was he looking for? What did he say about the mission of Jesus (30–35)?

3. What do you think Anna was praying for all those years in the temple? What did she recognize about the infant Jesus?

4. Luke omits any details about the flight to Egypt to save the child's life. In verses 39–40, Jesus and his family return to their hometown, Nazareth. How does Luke describe the childhood of Jesus?

Reflection

Jesus had good Jewish parents, so when the time was right, they took him to the temple to present him to the Lord.

"*Born under law*" (21–24; Gal. 4:4). Circumcision and purification customs after birth symbolized the cleansing of sin by blood and sacrifices. Although our Lord was without sin or guilt, he had to perform all the obligations of the Law and fulfill all righteousness (Matt. 3:15) in order to become the Savior his name proclaimed him to be (21).

"*The consolation of Israel*" is a delightful description of our Lord Jesus (25). Comforting is God's proper work (Isa. 51:3, 11–12). In the Old Testament God's comfort came to his people through his Word (Ps. 119:52, 76, 82) and his chosen prophets. But all looked forward to the Messiah, the greatest Comforter (Is. 61:1–2; Luke 4:18–19).

"*The redemption of Jerusalem*" (38) had to do not with the city itself, but its inhabitants (See Matt. 23:37). Jesus would become the Comforter of sinners by becoming their Redeemer from sin through the shedding of his own blood. Redemption is costly.

Both Simeon and Anna believed God would keep his promise to send the Messiah. That they recognized the infant Jesus, brought to the temple by his humble parents in fulfillment of prophecy, is as awesome as the angel choir announcing his birth to the shepherds.

My Response

Memory Point

Recite Key Verse 1 from memory and ponder what this truth must have meant to Anna and Simeon.

☐ PRAY to apply God's Word

Lord, help me to be as faithful in waiting for your second coming as Simeon and Anna were in awaiting your first coming . . .

8

☐ **PRAY for insight into God's Word**
I want to know your will for me today, Lord, and to understand more about you.

☐ **READ Luke 2:41–52**

☐ **MEDITATE on God's Word**

Discovery
1. From reading this passage, what can you discern about Jesus' family life?

Note: three days (46) probably means the third day after they had left Jerusalem the first time: a day's journey out, a day's journey back, finding Jesus on the third day.

2. What had Jesus been doing in the temple? Imagine the excitement of learning in the temple at Jerusalem as compared with opportunities in the small town of Nazareth.

3. What are the first recorded words of Jesus? What does this indicate about his growing awareness of his identity?

4. How does Luke describe Jesus' teen-age years (51–52)? Can that be said of your developing awareness of who you are?

Reflection

All Jewish males were required to attend the temple three times a year for the feasts of Passover, Pentecost, and Tabernacles (Exod. 23:17). As the Jews were scattered all over the Roman world, most made the effort to go to the temple at least annually. Joseph and Mary went regularly at Passover time. Our Lord probably visited Jerusalem at the age of twelve to be prepared for the *Bar Mitzvah* ceremony the following year—when, as a thirteen-year-old boy, he would join the religious community as a responsible member.

A unique relationship to God (49). The first recorded words of the Messiah were a recognition of his unique relationship of sonship to God and of the necessity of his being in his Father's house, going about his Father's business.

Perfect development. Our Lord's perfection at each stage of his early growth is evident. First he was a good listener, seizing the opportunity of Jerusalem's abundance of good teachers to ask questions (46). But observers were as much aware of his wisdom and understanding as of any help he received (47). He grew so that at every stage he fulfilled the will of God (52).

My Response

Memory Point

Look back over the studies you have done this far. How have they increased your awareness of the truth of Key Verse 1 (Luke 1:37)?

☐ PRAY to apply God's Word

Dear God, because of Jesus you are also my Father in heaven. Help me to be an eager learner of spiritual truths and to be a growing person—in favor with God and other people . . .

2/Preparation for the Good News
Luke 3:1–4:13

☐ **Introduction**

We know that both John the Baptist and the Lord Jesus Christ had a special mission. When do you think John became conscious of his mission in life? And what about Jesus' consciousness of who he really was?

We tend to think of these biblical characters, and of Jesus in particular, as having little in common with our humanity. Yet the Scripture says Jesus understands everything about us because he, too, was human (Heb. 2:14–18).

John the Baptist was probably an ordinary little boy growing up in the home of older parents, where he was taught the Scriptures and the hope of a coming Messiah. God was preparing him in every way to be his messenger, but there is no reason to think he was an odd little boy who wore a halo around his head. Luke tells us (3:1–3) that "the word of God came to John." We can't know for certain, but probably this was the time when John the Baptist began to realize what his task was. He was becoming the person God would use. He was ready to be that person when "the word of the Lord came to him."

Why is that important enough to mention? Because it reminds us that God has a purpose for us and our children who will come after us. It is important to be growing into the person God can use for his purpose.

Jesus too had a childhood very much like other boys and girls growing up in good Jewish homes. Surely Mary and Joseph taught him what the Scriptures said about the Messiah, but Luke 2:51 reminds us that he had to be obedient to his parents, just as we must be. And his parents were not perfect, just as we are not perfect parents and have not been raised by perfect parents.

When Jesus was thirty years old, his mission became clearer. The Bible doesn't say much about his self-realization, but you will read how "the word of the Lord" came to Jesus. God spoke from heaven at the time of his baptism. Immediately afterwards the Holy Spirit led Jesus into the wilderness, and for forty days he wrestled with the implications of his mission. The devil tried to dissuade him from carrying out God's purposes, but to no avail. He knew who he was and what he had come to do as God the Son in human form. Jesus returned to Galilee in the power of the Spirit, ready to begin three years of ministry, proclaiming that the kingdom of God had come and knowing that he would die for the sins of the world.

As you read the stirring accounts of the preparation of these two men, ask yourself if you have any sense of the mission the Lord is giving you. How does God want to use your life? The Key Verse for this section tells us what God desires.

☐ Key Verse 2: Luke 3:6
All mankind will see God's salvation.

☐ Outline of the Gospel of Luke

I. Birth and Childhood Narratives 1:1–2:52
  A. John's birth and mission foretold 1:1–25
  B. Jesus' birth and mission foretold 1:26–56
  C. Zechariah's blessing 1:57–80
  D. Jesus' birth 2:1–40
  E. The boy Jesus at the temple 2:41–52

II. Preparation for the Good News 3:1–4:13
  A. John the Baptist's ministry 3:1–14
  B. Jesus' baptism 3:15–23
  C. Jesus' temptation 4:1–13

III. Jesus in Galilee 4:14–9:45
  A. Jesus in Nazareth and Capernaum 4:14–44
  B. Jesus' call to faith 5:1–6:11
  C. Jesus' call and teaching of the Twelve 6:12–49
  D. Jesus' compassion 7:1–50
  E. Understanding Jesus' ministry 8:1–56
  F. Understanding who Jesus is 9:1–45

IV. Traveling toward Jerusalem 9:46–19:27
  A. Realities of discipleship 9:46–10:42
  B. Teaching about prayer 11:1–13
  C. Jesus' response to criticism 11:14–12:12
  D. Jesus' instructions to his disciples 12:13–12:59
  E. Call to repentance and faith 13:1–35
  F. Teaching about values 14:1–16:31
  G. Forgiveness and faith 17:1–19
  H. The coming kingdom 17:20–18:30
  I. Jesus nearing Jerusalem 18:31–19:27

V. Jesus in Jerusalem 19:28–21:38
  A. Triumphal entry 19:28–48
  B. Teaching in the temple area 20:1–21:4
  C. Signs of the end of the age 21:5–38

VI. Jesus' Last Hours with His Disciples 22:1–53
  A. The upper room 22:1–38
  B. In the garden 22:39–53

VII. Arrest and Crucifixion 22:54–23:56
  A. Denial and mockery 22:54–71
  B. Trial 23:1–25
  C. Crucifixion and burial 23:26–56

VIII. Resurrection 24:1–53
  A. Empty tomb 24:1–12
  B. Road to Emmaus 24:13–35
  C. Joyful disciples 24:36–53

9

☐ **PRAY for insight into God's Word**
Dear God, prepare my heart to hear your Word, so that "the way of the Lord" might be made ready in me.

☐ **READ Luke 3:1–14**

☐ **MEDITATE on God's Word**

Discovery
1. How does Luke's careful research document the beginning of John's ministry (1–2)? What significant facts does he give?

2. What was the message of John the Baptist? Notice his picturesque language. How can his exhortations be called "good news" (18)?

3. What did John demand of those who responded to his message? By doing so, what was he teaching about God's character?

4. What groups are mentioned among the questioners in verses 10–14? How did their different callings offer different temptations? How do John's words challenge your own life?

Reflection

The 400-year silence since Malachi, the last of the Old Testament prophets, was finally broken. John came as a prophet foretold by Malachi (Mal. 3:1) and attested by the fact that the word of God came to him (2). He came to a world of people ruled by Rome. Luke's careful documentation conveys the impression that this was a decisive event—John inaugurated God's mighty act of salvation, greater even than the Exodus.

John's mission was to get the hearts of people ready for the Messiah. "The King is coming," he said. "Get your lives straightened out." His message was a call for personal repentance from sin. Crooked ways must be made straight. God's salvation was about to be revealed.

Purity, not privilege (7–9). Notice how forthright John was. There was no mincing of words and scarcely a welcome for those who made the demanding journey to the Jordan. The Jews had trusted in their relationship to Abraham and an outward show of ritual; John saw that God set no store whatever on these.

"Fruit in keeping with repentance" (8, 10–14). The impact of John's ministry witnesses to:

—the convicting power of his Spirit-directed preaching.
—the condition of his contemporary society with oppressive taxation (12–13) and a corrupt, violent police force (14).

My Response

Memory Point

"All mankind will see God's salvation." If this is God's purpose in sending Christ, how can you, like John, be a messenger of this good news? Repeat Key Verse 2 several times throughout the day to remind yourself of God's purpose.

☐ PRAY to apply God's Word

Lord, show me the hypocrisy and wrong in my own life so that I may be ready for your gracious work in me . . .

10

☐ **PRAY for insight into God's Word**
Dear Lord, thank you for being willing to identify and live with sinners. Give me new insights as I study today.

☐ **READ Luke 3:15–23**

☐ **MEDITATE on God's Word**

Discovery
1. How did John answer those who wondered if he was the Christ? Read John 3:28–30 for further insight into John's view of himself. From John's description, what picture would the people have of Jesus?

2. Contrast the people's response to John's strong words (10–14) with Herod's response (19–20). What is your own response to exhortation?

3. Compare Luke's account of Jesus' baptism in verses 21–22 with Matthew 3:13–17. As Jesus begins his public ministry, how does he express his humanity? How is his uniqueness as the Son of God declared?

4. Jesus was in his thirties when he began his ministry. What aspects of life would he already have dealt with that underscore the truth of Hebrews 4:15? Glance through verses 24–38. Notice that Luke ends the genealogy with Adam, thus emphasizing that Jesus is the Savior not only of the Jews as Abraham's descendants, but of all humankind. Compare Matthew 1:1–2.

Reflection

Surely people were awaiting expectantly (15), for there was no greater hope for the Jew than the anticipation of the Messiah. John's ascetic way of life and his blunt teaching hardly fit into the popular Jewish concept of a messiah, however. John swiftly dispelled any doubts; he was merely the forerunner, shortly to be eclipsed by one so infinitely mighty that John considered himself unworthy to perform even the most menial task for him (16). Jesus' baptism would be not merely symbolic but effective, especially in its purifying effect (17). It may seem strange to describe such searching judgment as "good news" (18), but the blessings of salvation can never be experienced until sin has been dealt with.

In the same small corner of the ancient world was Herod (19–20), who, setting himself above God's law, had divorced his wife to marry his sister-in-law, misusing his power to silence opposition. Jesus, significantly, had no word to say to the man who had refused to take John's condemnation to heart (23:6–12).

Note the way Luke introduces the Lord's public ministry. There is no fanfare of trumpets to herald this world-shattering event: the Son of God enters almost unobtrusively. He humbles himself in baptism, he prays, and he is filled with God's Spirit. Is there a sense in which, following this pattern, we may share God's commendation (22) as joint-heirs with Christ (Rom. 8:17)?

My Response

Memory Point

Copy Key Verse 2 (Luke 3:6) on a 3x5 card and place it where you can see it often to memorize the words and the reference.

☐ PRAY to apply God's Word

Lord, your humility overwhelms me. Help me to grow to be more like you . . .

11

☐ **PRAY for insight into God's Word**
Father, thank you that Jesus was made a human being like me. Teach me today what I need to know about handling temptation in my life.

☐ **READ Luke 4:1–13**

☐ **MEDITATE on God's Word**

Discovery
1. Review what had happened at the Jordan River in 3:22. What was Jesus' condition when he went into the wilderness (1)?

2. When did the Devil begin to tempt Jesus? Would this have been a real temptation? How did Jesus handle it?

3. In view of what Jesus understood about his mission, why would the second and third offers of Satan be difficult temptations (5, 9)?

4. What does the way Jesus met *every* temptation tell you about the importance of Scripture in your own life? What can you do to increase your ability to handle Scripture in this way?

Reflection

These temptations were real to Jesus—otherwise the episode was a meaningless charade. We learn that:

Temptation originates from the Devil (2). This does not contradict James 1:12–15, where the emphasis is on the *person* who allows the Devil to control his life.

Even the Spirit-filled, Spirit-directed person (1) is vulnerable (1 Cor. 10:12).

The Devil's timing is expert. He often comes at a time of spiritual exaltation (after our Lord's baptism) or during physical weakness (after a long fast) with appropriate temptations.

Temptation may involve the misuse of God-given powers to satisfy our material needs, to effect a short cut to apparently legitimate goals (5–6), especially when it involves the bypassing of suffering (Matt. 16:21–23), or to gain popular applause. Even Scripture is distorted by Satan to lend apparent support (9–11).

The Bible is our best defense against Satan, for it makes God's will plain. To be effective, God's Word must be readily available, stored in our hearts.

Jesus was stronger, spiritually, because he overcame temptation (14; Heb. 2:18).

Victory is no guarantee of future immunity (13). A battle had been won, but the warfare continued.

My Response

Memory Point

Review the two Key Verses on your 3x5 cards and notice how they outline what you have studied this far.

☐ PRAY to apply God's Word

Pray the Lord's Prayer (Luke 11:2–4) . . .

3/Jesus in Galilee
Luke 4:14–9:45

☐ Introduction

What makes it so hard to go back to your hometown and try to tell people what you've become? Famous artists who perform around the world find themselves quaking and uneasy in front of the hometown crowd.

In the same way, family members are often the most difficult people to talk to about personal faith. We can speak to others about what Jesus means to us and what has been happening to us spiritually, but something about "having grown up there" makes us self-conscious before our relatives. Maybe the barrier comes because we think we know them too well, or think they know us too well. Whatever the reason, it's often easier to begin something new among strangers.

In this next section of Luke's gospel Jesus goes back to Nazareth where he had been brought up (4:16). After his wilderness experience he comes back to Galilee in the power of the Spirit, and news about him spreads throughout the whole countryside: "Local boy becomes preacher and teacher."

In his hometown he goes to the synagogue on the Sabbath day. Luke makes a point of telling us that Jesus was in the habit of doing this. They give him the scroll of the prophet Isaiah, and carefully he chooses the place to read. Every eye is on him, and they are listening intently. What has Jesus been doing that has brought such acclaim in other places?

Don't miss the excitement and drama of the moment. He reads a prophecy about the Messiah. It's a passage they all know, but when he finishes reading, Jesus says that the passage refers to himself and that he has come into the world to do what it says. There, he has done it. He has come back home and told the people who he is.

Their first reaction is amazement, and then someone thinks to ask, "Isn't this Joseph's son?" And when he chides them for their unbelief, these good hometown folks take him to the brow of a hill and are ready to throw him off the cliff! Jesus understands what it means to be rejected and misunderstood.

Does he give up? No, he stays in the region of Galilee. Notice all that he does: miracles, calling the disciples, teaching, confronting synagogue leaders concerning the proper observance of the Sabbath. Word continues to spread about his miracles and his teaching. People begin to see, "God has come to help his people." His reputation grows, but Jesus is a realist. He knows that wide acclaim is different from genuine belief.

Read this section as if you were one of the early disciples of Jesus. Traveling with Jesus and seeing what he does, gives you an experience of who he is and what he can do in human lives. Later he will ask you who you believe he really is. He will show you new things about his glory and tell you about his purpose in dying. You will begin to understand in new ways the truth of the Key Verse for this section.

Jesus in Galilee/Luke 4:14–9:45   **37**

☐ Key Verse 3: Luke 5:31–32
It is not the healthy who need a doctor, but the sick. I have not come to call the righteous, but sinners to repentance.

☐ Outline of the Gospel of Luke

I. Birth and Childhood Narratives *1:1–2:52*
   A. John's birth and mission foretold   *1:1–25*
   B. Jesus' birth and mission foretold   *1:26–56*
   C. Zechariah's blessing   *1:57–80*
   D. Jesus' birth   *2:1–40*
   E. The boy Jesus at the temple   *2:41–52*

II. Preparation for the Good News *3:1–4:13*
   A. John the Baptist's ministry   *3:1–14*
   B. Jesus' baptism   *3:15–23*
   C. Jesus' temptation   *4:1–13*

III. Jesus in Galilee *4:14–9:45*
   A. **Jesus in Nazareth and Capernaum**   *4:14–44*
   B. **Jesus' call to faith**   *5:1–6:11*
   C. **Jesus' call and teaching of the Twelve**   *6:12–49*
   D. **Jesus' compassion**   *7:1–50*
   E. **Understanding Jesus' ministry**   *8:1–56*
   F. **Understanding who Jesus is**   *9:1–45*

IV. Traveling toward Jerusalem *9:46–19:27*
   A. Realities of discipleship   *9:46–10:42*
   B. Teaching about prayer   *11:1–13*
   C. Jesus' response to criticism   *11:14–12:12*
   D. Jesus' instructions to his disciples   *12:13–12:59*
   E. Call to repentance and faith   *13:1–35*
   F. Teaching about values   *14:1–16:31*
   G. Forgiveness and faith   *17:1–19*
   H. The coming kingdom   *17:20–18:30*
   I. Jesus nearing Jerusalem   *18:31–19:27*

V. Jesus in Jerusalem *19:28–21:38*
   A. Triumphal entry   *19:28–48*
   B. Teaching in the temple area   *20:1–21:4*
   C. Signs of the end of the age   *21:5–38*

VI. Jesus' Last Hours with His Disciples *22:1–53*
   A. The upper room   *22:1–38*
   B. In the garden   *22:39–53*

VII. Arrest and Crucifixion *22:54–23:56*
   A. Denial and mockery   *22:54–71*
   B. Trial   *23:1–25*
   C. Crucifixion and burial   *23:26–56*

VIII. Resurrection *24:1–53*
   A. Empty tomb   *24:1–12*
   B. Road to Emmaus   *24:13–35*
   C. Joyful disciples   *24:36–53*

12

☐ **PRAY for insight into God's Word**

Father, as I study today about the beginning of Jesus' ministry, I pray you will give me a new understanding of the Good News.

☐ **READ Luke 4:14–30**

☐ **MEDITATE on God's Word**

Discovery

1. Where and how did Jesus begin his public ministry (14–15)?

2. What revelation about himself did he make in his hometown of Nazareth? What did he say about his mission? Contrast his message with that of John the Baptist.

3. What hindered Jesus' ministry in Nazareth (22–24)? Compare Mark 6:4–6. Look at the two illustrations Jesus used to prove his point in verses 25–27. What was the nationality of the widow? Of Naaman? (If you have a Bible map, look up Sidon and Syria.) What was Jesus indicating about the scope of his own ministry?

4. What made the difference between the opinion of the crowd in verses 28–29 and verse 22? Compare the third temptation Jesus faced in 4:9–11 with what the people tried to do in verse 29. What do you notice about Jesus' conduct in all of this? Do you want to be like him?

Reflection

Home is always the hardest place to gain appreciation (24). As the distinguished "local boy who made good," Jesus was invited to read the prophetic passage (17). His regular attendance at the synagogue, in spite of all its imperfections (16), surely rebukes the modern "I don't go to church because I get nothing out of it" attitude.

Whether the passage he read was a set portion, or personally selected, is uncertain, but the passage itself (Isa. 61:1-2) was highly significant. The words describe the Messiah's ministry to people in distress—the poor, the captive, the blind, and the oppressed. Jesus read the words and then sat down, thus taking the posture for preaching. With everyone now expectantly looking at him, Jesus said that *that moment* the prophecy was fulfilled. The words of Isaiah applied to the ministry Jesus was beginning. His was the day of salvation.

By his presence and teaching, the sifting, winnowing processes had begun. His neighbors' patronizing comments were coupled with doubts (23). Thinking they knew, they became ignorant; familiarity dulled their sensitivity. Jesus' illustrations concerning the bypassing of Israel (25-27) were ominous portents of the fate of his own people (John 1:11). Smugly complacent, ready to judge but not be judged, their reaction betrayed their injured pride and fickleness (28-30).

My Response

Memory Point

Copy Key Verse 3 (Luke 5:31-32) on a 3x5 card. In what way is the truth of this verse illustrated by Jesus' experience in today's reading?

☐ PRAY to apply God's Word

Help me to face any situation of rejection with the memory and love of you, Lord Jesus . . .

13

☐ **PRAY for insight into God's Word**
Lord, quiet my heart to think your thoughts and to be attentive to your Word.

☐ **READ Luke 4:31-44**

☐ **MEDITATE on God's Word**

Discovery
1. What was unique about Jesus' ministry? Look through the passage and write down your observations.

_____

2. What did the evil spirits seem to know about Jesus? (See James 2:19.)

_____

3. These verses account for one day in the life of Jesus. Notice the sequence of events as you observe how he spent his day. What was his secret in meeting daily demands?

_____

4. What compelling motive kept Jesus from staying in Galilee?

Reflection

Since Nazareth had rejected him, Jesus made his Galilean headquarters at Capernaum, probably in Simon Peter's home (38). In the packed 24-hour period described in these verses, Jesus touched four representative areas.

The synagogue (31–37). In a day when we are witnessing inexplicable powers of evil (which often demonstrate supernatural knowledge similar to that revealed here) we have grown less prone to dismiss demon possession than were earlier generations.

The home (38–39). A high fever normally leaves lingering debility. But when Christ heals, he does it perfectly, instantaneously. If you have been healed (spiritually or physically) by Christ, is your immediate reaction to *rise* and *serve?*

The town (40–41). When the Sabbath restriction was over, the sick could be carried to Jesus. Even in a crowd, he still manages to deal directly with the individual.

The surrounding area (42–44). We dare not be possessive, or restrict Christ's presence and power; he must be shared.

The secret of such a full life is in verse 42a. (Mark 1:35 adds to our understanding of this verse.) *Jesus made time* for communion with his Father, the source of his divine compassion (40), compulsion (43), and power (32, 36). Is our need for communion with the Father any less?

My Response

Memory Point

Read Key Verse 3 (Luke 5:31–32) twice today, stopping to pray for someone you know who is spiritually sick, in need of Jesus' healing.

☐ PRAY to apply God's Word

Lord, give me the sensitivity, the insight, and the power to meet the needs of others today.

14

☐ **PRAY for insight into God's Word**
Lord, make me as eager to hear the Word of God as were the people who crowded around Jesus in today's reading.

☐ **READ Luke 5:1-16**

☐ **MEDITATE on God's Word**

Discovery
1. Why do you think Jesus borrowed Simon's boat? Find three possible reasons.

2. Why do you think Simon, the fisherman, obeyed Jesus, the carpenter, when he gave fishing instructions (4–5)?

3. What more do you think Simon Peter realized about Jesus from his reaction in verse 8? Why did Simon and his partners leave their biggest catch behind (9–11)?

4. What did the leper believe about Jesus (12–16)? How did Jesus show his compassion (13)? His respect for existing laws (14)? His way of handling pressure (16)?

Reflection

Jesus ministered to *people*, and it didn't seem to matter to him whether the audience was large enough to require voice amplification (sound carries well over water), or one needy man who was an outcast of society.

Jesus and the multitude (1–11). Our Lord taught not only in the synagogue (4:31), but wherever people gathered together or worked (1). Sometimes established churches fall short in the area of outreach, expecting that needy people will come to *them*. Christ readily adapted to circumstances, using what was available (3). A courteous request (3) led to an authoritative command (4). Simon obeyed, though it clashed with his authority as an experienced fisherman. His awareness of Jesus' divine power was accompanied by a fearful realization of his own sinfulness. Is there a hint in verse 10 that our previous experience is used by Christ in the new life of discipleship? When these fishermen "left everything" (11), it included their biggest-ever catch. There was, and always is, greater satisfaction in following Christ.

Jesus and the individual (12–16). This man, who as a leper had no right to be in the city, did not doubt the *power* of Jesus, but doubted his *willingness* to heal. These doubts were quickly dispelled. Few incidents so reveal the compassion of Christ. He actually *touched* the leper, thereby incurring ritual defilement. His compassion overruled all such scruples—it was probably the first voluntary touch the leper had felt since he had been pronounced unclean.

My Response

Memory Point
Keep a copy of Key Verse 3 (Luke 5:31–32) at your kitchen table. Review it at each meal and read it aloud before you say grace.

☐ **PRAY to apply God's Word**
Lord Jesus, thank you for touching me, making me clean, and calling me to follow you . . .

15

☐ **PRAY for insight into God's Word**

Dear Father, let me see both the compassion and authority of Jesus in my own life as I study today.

☐ **READ Luke 5:17–26**

☐ **MEDITATE on God's Word**

Discovery

1. Describe the setting of this story. Who was present? (List 3 groups.) Where had they come from? Why were they there?

2. What did Jesus' words in verse 20 mean to the teachers of the law and the Pharisees? To the man who was paralyzed?

3. Why did Jesus begin with the forgiveness of sins? What was he proving about himself in the outcome of this encounter?

4. What was the response of the paralyzed man? The people who saw the miracle? How do you respond to being forgiven and healed?

Reflection

Luke records an increasing tide of opposition to Jesus, culminating in the fury of the religious leaders. How interesting is the varied reaction to his ever-increasing fame (15a)! Some responded in faith (15b), but the religious leaders came not to submit, but to assess (17). They were perfectly correct in their assertion that only God could forgive sins (21), but they failed to recognize the divine origin of Christ, who gave two further indications of his deity.

Healing, as well as forgiving sins, was God's prerogative. It was harder to claim that you could heal than it was to claim you could forgive sins, since the former could be proved (or disproved) immediately and objectively. In healing the crippled man, the power to forgive sins was also implicit.

Jesus described himself as "the Son of Man," a recognized Messianic title. Although these authorities "gave praise to God" (26), they did not really understand.

It is refreshing to turn to the healed man who glorified God because of a two-fold personal experience (25). Christ responded to the persistent faith of those who overcame difficulties by employing considerable initiative (19). They, as well as their crippled friend, surely received far more than they expected. Is there a parable in this?

My Response

Memory Point

Repeat Key Verse 3 (Luke 5:31–32) and meditate on its application to today's reading.

☐ PRAY to apply God's Word

Read 1 John 1:9 and apply its teaching. Then thank God that Jesus has authority to forgive your sins. Who can you bring to Jesus for forgiveness and healing, as the friends in this story did?

16

☐ **PRAY for insight into God's Word**
Show me today, dear Lord, something new about what it means to know you.

☐ **READ Luke 5:27–39**

☐ **MEDITATE on God's Word**

Discovery
1. What evidence of the reality of Levi's discipleship do you see in verses 27–29? How does your own discipleship compare with his?

2. Why did Jesus associate with "tax collectors and sinners"? What action and attitude does Jesus look for, according to verse 32?

3. What three illustrations did Jesus use to explain to the Pharisees that he was teaching something new, not just patching up Judaism (33–39)?

4. What keeps people from being open to change? In what ways do you (or others) protect yourself from new ideas?

Reflection

When Jesus called Levi (Matthew) his reaction was two-fold:

An immediate, sacrificial response—"he left everything" (28). Matthew's account (Matt. 9:9) significantly omits this. He knew that, in following Jesus, he had gained all, not lost everything, despite the fact that there could be no return for him after his "walkout."

He wanted to share his new Friend with his old associates (29–32). To the Pharisees, eating in such company, with its implication of fellowship and identification, resulted in "guilt by association." Jesus broke through this pedantry, and reached out to sinful, needy people. Note how these religious leaders talked to themselves (22) and to the disciples (30) before directly attacking Jesus himself (6:2). Self-righteousness, easy to detect in others, is hard to discern in ourselves, and harder to cure, for it blinds us to our need.

The relationship between Jesus and his disciples is glimpsed in verses 33–39. They were a happy group, unfettered by self-imposed fasts and patterns of prayer, although the Gospels make it abundantly clear that prayer *was* a vital part of their lives.

Jesus wanted the Pharisees to understand that what he had come to do and what he taught were radically different from their perceptions of religious life. "New wine" required new wineskins. Satisfaction with the status quo would keep them from tasting this "new wine" of salvation.

My Response

Memory Point

Memorize Key Verse 3 (Luke 5:31–32). Now make specific plans to spend time with someone you know who needs Jesus' healing. Call that person and plan a time to get together.

☐ PRAY to apply God's Word

Lord, give me Levi's enthusiasm in knowing you. Help me to share you with my friends and keep me in touch with people who need you . . .

17

☐ **PRAY for insight into God's Word**
Lord, help me to come to your Word with an open mind and a needy heart that I may learn from you.

☐ **READ Luke 6:1-11**

☐ **MEDITATE on God's Word**

Discovery
1. Lacking cafés or fast-food restaurants along the way, travelers in Bible times were permitted to hand-glean grain to satisfy their hunger (Deut. 23:25). Why did the Pharisees criticize Jesus and his disciples?

2. What point did Jesus make by giving the illustration from the Old Testament about David's action (1 Sam. 21:3–6)? What is Jesus' relationship to the Sabbath?

3. How did Jesus demonstrate his lordship over both disease and the Sabbath (6–11)?

4. How did Jesus reveal the intent of the Pharisees' hearts? According to Jesus, what are the choices for the Sabbath?

Reflection

Rules can only take care of outward behavior; they do not determine what is in the heart. Rules had become more important than people to the Pharisees, and Jesus spoke directly to the issue.

In the cornfield (1–5). The Sabbath, given for rest and remembrance (Exod. 20:8–11; Deut. 5:12–15), had become encrusted with ridiculous restrictions. Plucking and rubbing ears of grain was defined as reaping and threshing. Christ's reference to David showed that the Lord's anointed had authority to overrule God-given ordinances in the light of man's need. Jesus remains "Lord of the Sabbath." Our freedom from the law's letter is a *freedom to honor him,* not *carte blanche* to please ourselves.

In the synagogue (6–11). This was probably a contrived situation—the crippled man, his humanity and need forgotten, was a "plant" to trap Jesus. Jesus refused to be intimidated, however, and he took the initiative by bringing the man into the open (8) and by directly challenging the Pharisees and teachers (10). At first silent before Christ, they were voluble enough afterwards (11), furious because in their view he had broken the Sabbath and because they were unable to meet his challenge. How they could overlook a powerful, gracious work of healing, or the spirit of a passage like Isaiah 58 (with its demand for a humane, positive attitude toward fasting and Sabbath observance) is baffling. But there is nothing so blind as religious prejudice.

My Response

Memory Point
Review all three Key Verses from your 3x5 cards.

☐ PRAY to apply God's Word
Father God, keep me from misunderstanding your purposes and your compassion because of preconceived notions. Instead, give me the freedom to honor you with all my days . . .

18

☐ **PRAY for insight into God's Word**

Teach me what is really valuable, Lord—both by your example and by what you teach.

☐ **READ Luke 6:12–26**

☐ **MEDITATE on God's Word**

Discovery

1. On what basis did Jesus choose his disciples (12)? How do you make decisions?

2. Looking over the list of the Twelve Jesus chose, how would you characterize these men? What do you know about each of them? How did Simon the Zealot, for example, differ from Matthew (who is the Levi of 5:27)?

3. What contrasts do you observe in Jesus' teaching (20–26)?

4. What do you conclude about the difference between Christian values and worldly values? What is the difference in rewards?

Reflection

It's no small thing to choose the people who are going to carry on what you begin. How does anyone go about such an awesome task? Notice how Jesus did it.

The call of the disciples (12–16). When we consider the Lord at prayer, we are invariably rebuked. Prayer permeated his life, especially in times of crisis (Matt. 14:23; 26:36). There is an element of mystery in *the Son of God* needing to pray, to "keep in step," to ascertain the will of his Father. But if prayer was essential for him, how much more is it for us?

Jesus' choice of disciples was vital, for it involved the future leadership of the church. Since there was a "great crowd of disciples" (17), many were possibly disappointed. But whether chosen or not, the ultimate responsibility was (and still is) his. We can trust him, for he makes no mistakes.

The message to the disciples (20). Here in a large and needy crowd attracted from a radius of about 100 miles (17), Jesus concentrates on the disciples. The two-fold reference to the prophets (23, 26) implies that the disciples were the successors to Israel's great prophets. They were God's spokesmen to a generation that would reject them as their forefathers did the prophets.

My Response

Memory Point

Repeat Key Verse 3 (Luke 5:31–32) from memory. Follow up on contacts you have made with people who are spiritually sick. Have you introduced them to Jesus?

☐ PRAY to apply God's Word

Dear Lord Jesus, remind me today of heavenly values and keep me from being caught in the snares of this world. Teach me what it means to "seek first the kingdom of heaven" . . .

19

□ **PRAY for insight into God's Word**
Lord, as your Holy Spirit teaches me, touch my heart and mind in ways that make me more like Jesus.

□ **READ Luke 6:27-38**

□ **MEDITATE on God's Word**

Discovery
1. List the positive actions and attitudes (look for verbs) that Jesus says should characterize the life of his followers (27-31).

2. What is Jesus' reasoning (32-36) for this radical behavior? Whose example are we to follow?

3. Put the teaching of verses 37-38 in your own words.

4. What actions and attitudes do you need to change in order to obey these words of Jesus? Be specific and personal.

Jesus in Galilee/Luke 4:14–9:45

Reflection

Verse 27 probably marks the point where Jesus includes the wider company of bystanders (See 7:1). The same principles continue, but with a wider application.

Christ's commands, however, are not easy. The natural man seeks to hit back hard. As Christians we may be guilty of a sub-Christian attitude that follows the letter of the law only. We may show outward forms of submission or forgiveness when our real intentions are to "heap coals of fire" on the heads of our adversaries. Or we may plead that these commands couldn't possibly be implemented in *our* particular trouble-spot. Remember that Jesus was talking to people in occupied territory, under the iron rule of Rome, suffering extortionate taxation.

One is reminded here of Paul's great psalm on love (1 Cor. 13). Christ's life and teaching was Paul's model. Here is love that never retaliates, is never resentful, and is always reaching out with full hands, even to enemies. This is unrestricted love without selfish motivation, not governed by its object, not self-determinative, but *ruled solely by reference to God*. To achieve this we need God himself indwelling us, and this is precisely what he promises (Eph. 3:14–21).

My Response

Memory Point

Repeat Key Verse 3 (Luke 5:31–32) and meditate on its importance in the life of a disciple.

☐ PRAY to apply God's Word

Pray through this passage, asking God to help you change in ways where you think you need help . . .

20

☐ **PRAY for insight into God's Word**
Lord Jesus, give me a humble, listening heart as I read your words today.

☐ **READ Luke 6:39-49**

☐ **MEDITATE on God's Word**

Discovery
1. What care must a pupil take in choosing a teacher (39-40)? Find three ideas.

2. What humorous picture did Jesus use to make a serious point about hypocrisy in verses 41-42?

3. How did Jesus point out the consistency between "source and product" in verses 44-45? How does this relate to your conclusions from questions 1 and 2?

4. What is the great inconsistency in verse 46? How did Jesus illustrate the character of such a person? Does your life reflect Jesus' lordship? How?

Reflection

In today's study Jesus gives requirements for those who would be disciples and influence others.

You must See (39–42). There is serious intent in Christ's humorous satire. Many of us have been subjected to:
—the person whose knowledge is mainly ignorance and who leads others astray (39)
—the student who, inflated by a little knowledge, despises his teacher (40)
—the person who, insensitive to his own glaring faults, thinks that he can get away with any criticism, providing he prefaces his remarks with *"Brother..."* (41–42). To gain spiritual sight demands both sensitivity and humility.

You must Be (43–45). The test of time produces fruit of one kind or another and what is *within* will ultimately show. Since character determines conduct, the heart must be sound and well-stocked.

You must Do (46–49). The test of experience reveals the basic stability (or instability) of a person's life. Here our Lord speaks to the nominal, uncommitted follower, who goes along with him but is not really with him. Adversity always upsets such a person. In contrast, the "doer of the word" (James 1:22–25) gives wise thought to future dangers and prepares for them by strenuous present effort. The Greek verb used in "laid the foundation" (48) indicates continuous, persistent effort. This story warns about the testing time within this life, but there is also a future testing time. (See 1 Cor. 3:10–15, and note *the only enduring foundation.*)

My Response

Memory Point

Review Key Verse 3 (Luke 5:31–32) again today, thanking God that he accepts needy people as they are.

☐ PRAY to apply God's Word

Lord, it's obvious that if I really do believe you are the Lord, then I must listen to what you say and do it. Please nudge me any time I choose to build my ideas or plans on soft sand instead of on *the foundation* of who you are . . .

21

☐ **PRAY for insight into God's Word**
Dear Father, teach me something new about my own faith in you today as I read your Word.

☐ **READ Luke 7:1–10**

☐ **MEDITATE on God's Word**

Discovery
1. Look up the meaning of *centurion* in a dictionary. What was the nationality of this centurion?

2. Why were the Jewish elders willing to be his messengers (4–5)? What words come to your mind to describe the centurion?

3. What do you think the centurion believed about Jesus? Why do you think he changed his request of verse 3 to the message of verses 6 and 7?

4. What do you believe about the authority of Jesus? What areas of your life do you need to submit to his authority?

Reflection

When Jesus shows amazement (9) we must take notice. In fact there are several surprising things here:

—It was highly unusual for a Roman officer of such rank to show *concern for a mere slave*.

—It was unique for a *Roman officer to be commended* so warmly by local Jewish authorities (3–4). Apparently the centurion was not a proselyte, but he had a genuine desire to help (5).

—It was, of course, *the centurion's faith* that caused Christ to marvel. There was faith in Israel, like that of the disciples, who left all to follow Jesus. But in the centurion's case there was a new dimension, an unusual perception, which even those who were close to the Lord only gradually attained. The centurion had not met Jesus personally, but he recognized an authority that eclipsed his own. His absolute faith and acceptance of that authority left no room for any doubt, and for him the added security of Jesus' personal presence was unnecessary (6–8).

—This awareness led to *the centurion's remarkable humility*. To the Jews he seemed worthy (4); in the light of Christ's life he realized his own complete unworthiness (6–7).

My Response

Memory Point
Review Key Verse 3 (Luke 5:31–32) and note how it applies to the centurion.

☐ PRAY to apply God's Word
Lord Jesus, give me a fresh awareness of your authority in the daily events of my life . . .

22

☐ **PRAY for insight into God's Word**

Lord Jesus, show me who you are in new ways today so that I might know you better and trust you more.

☐ **READ Luke 7:11-23**

☐ **MEDITATE on God's Word**

Discovery

1. What description and phrases (11-15) reveal the heart-felt concern of Jesus?

2. What words would you use to describe the kind of person Jesus is? How does your response to Jesus compare with that of the people (16-17)?

3. How did Jesus' ministry differ from that of John the Baptist? (Review 3:7-18.) Why might Jesus' popularity have been confusing to John? Look back to 3:20 as a reminder of John's situation.

4. How did Jesus assure John about his identity? What would this have meant to John? (Review 4:16-21.)

Reflection

In today's study we see a tender-hearted Savior and a confused disciple.

Jesus' growing popularity (11–17). A two-fold tragedy confronted Christ—not only had the widow lost her sole means of support, but her family line faced extinction—a tragedy in Israel, with its strong corporate and hereditary sense. A "large crowd" (12) of mourners witnessed this miracle, and, not surprisingly, Jesus' fame spread abroad (16–17). Luke "slips" momentarily, using the title *the Lord* for the first time (13). This descriptive phrase was not used until after Jesus' death, but, reminded here of the Lord of life and death, it is appropriate that Luke should use this absolute, reverent title.

John's faltering faith (18–23). Did John expect to be a political, messianic figure, ridding the land of its Roman overlords—a view shared by the disciples (24:21; Acts 1:6)? The context (18) suggests that it was the very popularity of Jesus that caused offense (23), perhaps linked with his lack of scorching condemnation. No doubt the psychological pressures of imprisonment were considerable, and John wisely referred his doubts to the Lord. Using the prophecies of Isaiah 29:18 and 35:4–6, Jesus claimed messiahship, and John would have been discerning enough to realize that the overall context was Isaiah's concept of the *Suffering Servant.*

My Response

Memory Point

Review all three Key Verses. Remember John's part in giving needy people an awareness of Jesus. Are you doing your part?

☐ PRAY to apply God's Word

Lord Jesus, help me to be like John, bringing my honest doubts before you, so that I may be a genuine believer.

23

☐ **PRAY for insight into God's Word**

Lord, it's so easy to be distracted by the details of living. I want to have a hearing heart. Help me to listen to you today, I pray.

☐ **READ Luke 7:24–35**

☐ **MEDITATE on God's Word**

Discovery

1. What tribute does Jesus give to John? Notice what he says John is *not*. What two words in verses 26–27 describe John's ministry?

2. How can it be that those who are least in the kingdom of God are even greater than John? Put John's message in one word. Put Jesus' message in one word. Does this help you understand the position of those who enter the kingdom proclaimed by John?

3. Contrast the attitude of those who responded to John's ministry and those who did not (29–30).

4. How did Jesus emphasize the inconsistency of the scribes' and the Pharisees' response to John and to himself (31–35)?

Reflection

Lest his mild rebuke (23) be taken as a rejection of John, our Lord sets his great forerunner in his true perspective. The forthright John could never have been described as a fickle character (24), nor as a cultured dandy (25). To call him "a prophet" (26) placed him in exalted company, but John was more than this. There were many prophets, but only one herald, who immediately prepared Christ's way (27)—herein lay John's uniqueness. Although languishing in prison, he was no failure. Jesus immediately brings in a new dimension. He puts John into historical perspective. John came to announce the kingdom, which now has become a reality. And the least person in the kingdom is greater than John, not because of any personal qualities, but because he or she belongs to the kingdom. The kingdom of God, entered by the new birth (John 3:3) gives each believer a new, privileged status.

Two levels of response (29–35). Those with a sense of need, who had consistently responded to God's revelation through both John and Jesus, were "in the family" (35), rejoicing in the outworking of the wise, divine plan. But the self-righteous Pharisees were perpetually out of step, perversely finding hollow reasons for rejecting God's advances (33–34). They acted like tired children too irritable to play (32). Both groups had equal opportunity, but as one kept advancing, the rejection of the other became even more firmly entrenched. Why was this? Does 5:31–32 provide a clue?

My Response

Memory Point

Repeat Key Verse 3 (Luke 5:31–32) from memory. What have you learned from this verse?

☐ PRAY to apply God's Word

Dear Father in heaven, keep me from being proud and opinionated like the Pharisees in today's reading. Give me first a repentant spirit and then a joyful spirit because I am included in the kingdom of God . . .

24

☐ **PRAY for insight into God's Word**
Dear Father, use your Word today to reveal any hypocrisy in me, and help me to be more like Jesus.

☐ **READ Luke 7:36–50**

☐ **MEDITATE on God's Word**

Discovery
1. What do you know about Simon from this story? What judgment did he make about Jesus?

2. What do you know about the woman from the story?

3. Why did Jesus tell Simon a parable? Contrast Simon and the woman in their consciousness of personal need.

4. Why does self-sufficiency and pride shut a person off from God? See 1 Timothy 1:15 and note how Paul, a great man of faith, viewed himself. How do you see yourself before God?

Jesus in Galilee/Luke 4:14–9:45

Reflection

The scene of this story is the open courtyard of the house of Simon, the Pharisee. During warm weather, meals would have been served there, with the guests reclining on low couches around the table. It was the custom that when a Rabbi was visiting such a house, others could come in to listen. That explains the presence of the woman. She is nameless (to us) and is typical of a vast number who found help and healing from the Savior. This woman is often confused with Mary Magdalene, whom we do not meet until 8:2.

In the light of increasing Pharisaic opposition, it is remarkable that Simon invited Jesus into his home. Curiosity may have played a part, but it was a half-hearted and condescending welcome. He could not bring himself to stoop to the level of performing the normal courtesies toward guests (44), and his thinly-veiled skepticism shows through in verse 39, with its inference that Jesus was not a prophet. Note his grudging admission as he recognized himself in the parable (43). His trouble was that he had scant awareness of forgiveness (47), probably because of his basic self-righteousness.

But if Jesus was only half-welcome, the intruding woman was most unwelcome as, overcome with deep emotion, she gave open expression of gratitude (37–38). Love that stems from an awareness of forgiveness linked with faith (50) is extravagant and sacrificial. Would you be nearer in spirit to her—or to Simon?

My Response

Memory Point

How does Simon illustrate the truth of Key Verse 3 (Luke 5:31–32)?

☐ **PRAY to apply God's Word**

Lord, how easy it is to be like Simon, proud and self-righteous! Help me to see the beauty of the woman's response of love and humility. Help me to see how much I have been forgiven so that I might love you much . . .

25

☐ **PRAY for insight into God's Word**
"Your word is a lamp to my feet and a light for my path" (Ps. 119:105). Make this true for me today, dear Lord.

☐ **READ Luke 8:1–15**

☐ **MEDITATE on God's Word**

Discovery
1. What observations can you make about the support group that traveled with Jesus (1–3)?

2. What was happening in Jesus' ministry, according to verse 4?

3. In your own words describe Jesus' interpretation of the seed sown on the path, on rocky soil, among the thorns, and on good soil. How do parables both hide and reveal truth?

4. What kind of soil characterizes your own heart? What three verbs in verse 15 give clues about how to grow in the Christian life?

Reflection

Among the lessons from this familiar parable (4–15) note:

The sower must not lose heart. How discouraging such waste might have seemed. Some seed never had a chance (5, 12), being trampled by materialistic values or hardened into insensitivity. Some seed was received enthusiastically and grew rapidly until a basically shallow nature reasserted itself at the first sign of trial (6, 13). The third group's failure was the hardest for the sower to bear, for there was real growth potential. But a lack of separation and slackness in discipline made immaturity inevitable (7, 14). The fruitfulness of the fourth group (8, 15), however, made it all worthwhile.

The seed must be broadcast. It would seem good sense to be more selective, concentrating on the "soil" where good harvest is more likely. But we do not know the precise degree of response of any individual, and surprising results can come from the most unlikely.

The soil can be changed. God works miracles—breaking hardened hearts, transforming shallowness, stripping the cluttered lives of the preoccupied, and implanting a new dedication. The seed can produce fruit.

My Response

Memory Point

Review Key Verse 3 (Luke 5:31–32) and think about how it is illustrated by the parable of the sower. Thank God for calling *you* to repentance.

☐ PRAY to apply God's Word

Lord Jesus, thank you that you sow seeds of truth generously in our hearts by your Holy Spirit. Make my heart honest and good, so that I may receive your Word and grow a crop pleasing to you . . .

26

☐ **PRAY for insight into God's Word**

Lord, continue to show me the importance of hearing your Word and listening to what you say.

☐ **READ Luke 8:16–25**

☐ **MEDITATE on God's Word**

Discovery

1. Compare the *purpose* of sowing seed (8) and lighting a lamp (16).

2. Verses 16–18 seem to contain three separate sayings. How do these three ideas relate to each other, and how do they emphasize what Jesus taught in the parable of the sower?

3. From verses 19–21, what was of primary importance to Jesus? How was he expanding his family relationships?

4. In verses 22–25, what observations can you make about Jesus' words and behavior? About the disciples'? How does this account encourage your faith?

Reflection

Hearing and doing (18, 21) are intimately connected with the parable of the sower. The first (16–18) deals with a thwarted purpose. Just as seed should bear fruit, so light is meant to shine. Truth is given so that it may be revealed in our witness, and so that others, taking note, may be drawn to the One who illumines us. The second (19–21) in no way discounts the value of family relationships, as the gospel record of Christ's attitude to his family makes clear. But Mark 3:21, 31–35 shows that his relatives felt that he was going too far, almost accusing him of "religious mania." Are we prepared to be misunderstood because we, like Jesus, are passionate in doing the Father's will? Closer than any blood tie is this fellowship with Christ which shares God's loving heart and dynamic outreach.

A faith that faltered (22–25). It is easy to criticize the disciples, but this was no ordinary storm, and these men were no strangers to the dangerous, swiftly changing moods of this sea. Probably we would have been petrified with fear. And yet, when the Lord said, "Let us go across to the other side . . . ," could there have been any possibility of *not* arriving? Like most of us, the disciples came slowly and painfully to that awareness of the Son of God that excludes questionings and outbursts of complaint.

My Response

Memory Point

As you move among people today, think of how Key Verse 3 (Luke 5:31–32) applies to all those you meet.

☐ PRAY to apply God's Word

Dear Lord Jesus, you are looking for people who listen, hearing what you are saying. Keep me from being superficial or glib in my relationship with you. Help me to *hear* and to *do* . . .

27

☐ **PRAY for insight into God's Word**

Lord Jesus, show me something new about your power in human lives as I read and meditate today.

☐ **READ Luke 8:26-39**

☐ **MEDITATE on God's Word**

Discovery

1. Describe the man Jesus met when he stepped ashore. What had his life been like? What courage did Jesus show in facing him?

2. What did the demons recognize about the person and power of Jesus?

3. What changes did Jesus' healing bring to the man? What commission did Jesus give him?

4. Why did the townspeople ask Jesus to leave? What did this show about their values?

Reflection

Why were these people so afraid (34, 36–37)? After all, the source of their earlier fear, this demon-possessed man with abnormal strength and behavior, had been dealt with.

Did the economic loss of the swine upset them? The point that pigs were unclean animals is not valid, since this area was part of the Decapolis, a *Gentile* area. Certainly these men overlooked a work of grace. If a person is of more value than many sparrows (Matt. 10:31), was not the maniac's total restoration worthwhile?

More likely it was shattering for these Gentiles to be confronted with the power and presence of God. It is never a light thing to be in God's presence: Adam and Eve hid themselves (Gen 3:8), Isaiah felt that he was doomed (Isa. 6:5), and even Peter urged the Lord to depart (Luke 5:8–9). Origen recorded a statement attributed to Jesus that is certainly apt: "He who is near Me is near the fire."

So they asked Jesus to leave (37), and he *never forces himself* on anyone (compare Rev. 3:20). But a comparison with Mark 7:31–8:10 and Matthew 15:29–31 shows that he returned later, welcomed enthusiastically by great crowds. We cannot be certain to what extent the testimony of the ex-maniac whom Jesus sent home was responsible for this changed attitude. But they, above all, would appreciate the transformation, and, given time to ponder, would realize that *God was responsible* (39).

My Response

Memory Point

Review all three Key Verses. Recite them to a friend or someone in your home.

☐ PRAY to apply God's Word

Lord, help me to share with those closest to me what you have done for me. Keep the wonder of being accepted and forgiven by you fresh in my mind . . .

28

☐ **PRAY for insight into God's Word**
Lord Jesus, as I walk with you through the events of your life in what I read today, make yourself and your power real to me.

☐ **READ Luke 8:40–56**

☐ **MEDITATE on God's Word**

Discovery
1. Compare Jairus's need with the woman's need. What would the social reputation of each be?

2. Why do you think Jesus made a public issue of being "touched" by someone, when the crowds were pressing around him? What would this mean to the woman in her relationship to others? In her relationship to Jesus?

3. Meanwhile, what had happened at Jairus's home? How did Jesus immediately comfort the father?

4. What do you learn about Jesus' sensitivity to human need from the way he raised the dead girl and from his confrontation with the woman in the crowd?

Reflection

"Someone touched me . . ." (46). What will be the outcome of your Bible reading and prayer today? These two miracles doubtless remind us of the Savior's availability, gentleness, and power, but *we can take this for granted,* and a "quiet time" may become a mere formality. If we hope to be better equipped to meet today's challenges, then we too must reach out in faith and "touch" the Lord. There may have been an element of superstition, but basically this woman had real faith, and Jesus responded to it. People were pressing in around Jesus (42), and she was weakened by long illness, but *deep need always lends strength.* Note how the Lord readily distinguished between the physical pressure of the masses and the woman's slight touch of faith. Augustine comments, "Flesh presses; faith touches."

The needy person can *still* touch Jesus. His humanity, shared with us, ensures his sensitivity to our need; his deity guarantees his availability and his power to help (Heb. 4:15). *He knows* the way you take (Job 23:10); he knows your particular problems. You can reach out to him in the feebleness of your faith, without pretense, empty and hungry. You can rely on him to meet you, for he still knows the touch of needy faith and responds to it.

My Response

Memory Point
Apply Key Verse 3 (Luke 5:31–32) to today's reading, repeating it aloud.

☐ PRAY to apply God's Word
Lord Jesus, help me to reach out and touch you for my own needs. Make me aware of your presence throughout each event of this day . . .

29

☐ **PRAY for insight into God's Word**

Holy Spirit, thank you that you are my teacher. Give me fresh insight into this passage as I study today.

☐ **READ Luke 9:1–17**

☐ **MEDITATE on God's Word**

Discovery

1. In expanding his ministry in Galilee, what two-fold commission did Jesus give the Twelve? What were their resources as they went?

2. What evidence do you find in verses 7–9 of the effectiveness and extent of their ministry?

3. In verses 10–17, what further insights do you get about Jesus' concern for human need? About his power to provide for needs?

4. What did the disciples learn about Jesus from the way he fed 5,000 people? What do you learn?

Reflection

Since this was the first time that the disciples had served in this particular ministry, observe how Jesus dealt with them (1–6). Note the basic requirement of any servant of Christ—to be called, equipped, and specifically sent (1–2). Their mandate was clear: to set Christ's coming in the perspective of God's redemptive plan, and to heal (2, 6). We ought not to limit the healing ministry; obviously it related primarily to physical healing, and this power is still to be exercised today. But we are doing Christ's work if we seek to heal all hurts and divisions.

The end of the story (10–17) is equally instructive, highlighting *the need for Christian workers themselves to get apart with Christ.* (Mark 6:31 makes clearer the intention of rest and retreat.) Time spent with him renews our fellowship, vision, and resources.

Our Lord's attitude toward the intrusive crowd (11) suggests *the need to give ourselves completely* when there is demand on our time and ability. When we give, we do not lose.

Christ's concern for the people and his provision for their physical needs illustrate again for us *the need to trust him completely, even when circumstances seem to pose an impossible problem.*

My Response

Memory Point

Repeat Key Verse 3 (Luke 5:31–32). What do you see of Jesus' compassion in this verse that reminds you of today's reading?

☐ PRAY to apply God's Word

Lord Jesus, thank you for caring for both the physical and spiritual needs of people. Help me to be like you in your concerns . . .

30

☐ **PRAY for insight into God's Word**

Help me, Lord, to make a clear statement today about who you are and what I want our relationship to be.

☐ **READ Luke 9:18–27**

☐ **MEDITATE on God's Word**

Discovery

1. Jesus asked the disciples, "Who do the crowds say I am?" Compare their answer with the reports that reached Herod (7).

2. Jesus pressed for a personal response. What was the significance of Peter's answer? What is your response to Jesus' question?

3. What four important truths about his future as *the Christ* (Messiah) did Jesus share with the disciples?

4. How must a disciple follow his master (23–26)? What laws of spiritual life did Jesus give in verses 24 and 26?

Reflection

Jesus' question gives his followers an important opportunity to declare their personal attitude and response to him—something we must do also.

Knowledge of Christ is always a personal discovery. Peter spoke for all the disciples when he answered, "The Christ of God." Peter recognized Jesus as the Deliverer for whom the people of God so long had been looking. This was not a human discovery, but a revelation from God (see Matthew 16:17).

But neither he nor the people understood all that being *Messiah* meant. That is why Jesus warned them not to tell anyone. The people wanted a political deliverer and would have pressured him into that role as Messiah. They would have missed what he was teaching. He *had to* suffer. It was a divine necessity. The cross was his vocation. He offered no easy discipleship; indeed his pathway of suffering and rejection had to be accepted by his followers. This element so upset his disciples that they missed completely the glorious promises of his resurrection and triumphant second advent. The events at Calvary, the empty tomb, and Pentecost were needed before they (and we) could fully understand.

My Response

Memory Point

Repeat Key Verse 3 (Luke 5:31–32). What does it imply about who Jesus is?

☐ PRAY to apply God's Word

Teach me, Lord, the meaning of being your disciple. Help me not to be ashamed of confessing you before others . . .

31

☐ **PRAY for insight into God's Word**
Dear Lord, help me to be fully awake and aware, so that I may see who you really are as I spend this time with you today.

☐ **READ Luke 9:28–45**

☐ **MEDITATE on God's Word**

Discovery
1. Jesus was about to go to Jerusalem to die for humankind. What would his experience on the mountaintop have meant to him? What did Jesus, Moses, and Elijah talk about?

2. What observation did Peter make about the event?

3. What special anointing did Jesus receive from his Father? What would this experience mean for the disciples as they faced the future?

4. Contrast the triumph of Jesus' miracle in verses 37–43 with what he told his disciples in verses 44–45. In view of what they had experienced in the last few days, why was this so hard for the disciples to understand?

Reflection

While the Transfiguration would strengthen Jesus himself, its main purpose was to encourage the disciples. Christ's prophecy of suffering, rejection, and death (22) could have disillusioned them, and soon a great testing time would batter their faith. If their Master needed any vindication in their eyes, it was fully given through:

The witness of the Old Testament, attested by Moses and Elijah, the representatives of the Law and the Prophets respectively. Their presence was uniquely fitting. Both had shaped the pattern of Israel's hope; both had experienced divine encounters on Sinai's mountaintop.

The supernatural witness of the Father (34–35). Despite the many unmistakable proofs of Jesus' authority as God's Son, Peter (and the others) would remember this evidence of the Father's complete assurance throughout their ministries (see 2 Peter 1:16–18).

My Response

Memory Point

Review the three Key Verses. How does today's study apply to Key Verse 2 (Luke 3:6)?

☐ PRAY to apply God's Word

Lord, what an experience Peter, James, and John had on the mountain! Yet they almost missed it because they were sleepy. Oh, Father God, help me to be awake to see your glory in Christ Jesus . . .

4/Traveling toward Jerusalem
Luke 9:46–19:27

☐ Introduction

A. J. Cronin, a medical doctor and well-known author, tells of a dedicated public health nurse he knew when he practiced medicine. For twenty years she served a large district in England as the first level of available medical help. Even after being on duty all day, she took urgent night calls with a patience and cheerfulness that always amazed Dr. Cronin. Her salary was inadequate for the kind of work she was doing; her hours were impossible; the stress of the job was unrelieved. One day Dr. Cronin protested to her, "Why don't you make them pay you more? God knows you are worth it!"

"If God knows I'm worth it," she answered, "that's all that matters to me."

That attitude strikes us as unusual in this day of employment benefit packages and short work-weeks. But it is precisely this kind of radical perspective that Jesus asks of his disciples."

As he travels toward Jerusalem, Jesus gives his followers one adventure after another so that they can see in action who he is and what he can do. Over and over he shows them what is valuable and what it means to follow him. The Key Verse for this section (Luke 14:27) serves as a summary of what Jesus tries to help his disciples understand: "And anyone who does not carry his cross and follow me cannot be my disciple."

Christ is still taking people on adventures with himself, showing us who he is and what he can do if we will trust him. We have an advantage over the disciples because we have the Scriptures. We can read Luke's gospel and be instructed again and again. That's the whole point of studying a book like *Luke*—to see who Jesus is and get a fresh look at what he can do in human lives. He is still looking for genuine disciples who are interested in building the kingdom of God.

This section is called "Traveling toward Jerusalem," but that does not mean that Jesus is taking a straight route to that city. He seems to go in and out of Jerusalem and travels to many areas of Judea. His official entrance into Jerusalem comes at the end of this section and means the culmination of the events of his life as he is arrested and put on trial.

That makes the teaching of this section all the more important. Jesus knows his time is limited. What is he trying to teach his disciples in the time he has left? Keep looking, as you study, because the answer is for today's disciples as well.

☐ Key Verse 4: Luke 14:27
And anyone who does not carry his cross and follow me cannot be my disciple.

☐ Outline of the Gospel of Luke

I. Birth and Childhood Narratives   1:1–2:52
   A. John's birth and mission foretold   1:1–25
   B. Jesus' birth and mission foretold   1:26–56
   C. Zechariah's blessing   1:57–80
   D. Jesus' birth   2:1–40
   E. The boy Jesus at the temple   2:41–52

II. Preparation for the Good News   3:1–4:13
   A. John the Baptist's ministry   3:1–14
   B. Jesus' baptism   3:15–23
   C. Jesus' temptation   4:1–13

III. Jesus in Galilee   4:14–9:45
   A. Jesus in Nazareth and Capernaum   4:14–44
   B. Jesus' call to faith   5:1–6:11
   C. Jesus' call and teaching of the Twelve   6:12–49
   D. Jesus' compassion   7:1–50
   E. Understanding Jesus' ministry   8:1–56
   F. Understanding who Jesus is   9:1–45

IV. Traveling toward Jerusalem   9:46–19:27
   A. Realities of discipleship   9:46–10:42
   B. Teaching about prayer   11:1–13
   C. Jesus' response to criticism   11:14–12:12
   D. Jesus' instructions to his disciples   12:13–12:59
   E. Call to repentance and faith   13:1–35
   F. Teaching about values   14:1–16:31
   G. Forgiveness and faith   17:1–19
   H. The coming kingdom   17:20–18:30
   I. Jesus nearing Jerusalem   18:31–19:27

V. Jesus in Jerusalem   19:28–21:38
   A. Triumphal entry   19:28–48
   B. Teaching in the temple area   20:1–21:4
   C. Signs of the end of the age   21:5–38

VI. Jesus' Last Hours with His Disciples   22:1–53
   A. The upper room   22:1–38
   B. In the garden   22:39–53

VII. Arrest and Crucifixion   22:54–23:56
   A. Denial and mockery   22:54–71
   B. Trial   23:1–25
   C. Crucifixion and burial   23:26–56

VIII. Resurrection   24:1–53
   A. Empty tomb   24:1–12
   B. Road to Emmaus   24:13–35
   C. Joyful disciples   24:36–53

32

☐ **PRAY for insight into God's Word**

Dear Lord, thank you for caring so much about the small details of my life and for teaching me so patiently. Help me as I study today to see new truth.

☐ **READ Luke 9:46–62**

☐ **MEDITATE on God's Word**

Discovery

1. What personal insecurities did the disciples reveal about themselves in verses 46–55?

2. What lessons did they learn from Jesus as he dealt with their reactions?

3. Compare the three men on the road (57–62). What excuses kept each one from truly following Jesus?

4. Put the meaning of verse 62 in your own words. How would you define discipleship from this verse?

Reflection

Verse 51 is pivotal in this section. In light of Christ's unflinching commitment:

Notions of human greatness perish (46–48). Although Jesus modeled sacrificial service, his disciples were woefully slow to learn. (The same argument about greatness comes again in Luke 22:24.) People naturally jostle for pre-eminence, but Christ's followers must stoop.

Our attitude toward others broadens (49–50). The disciples' recent failure (38–40) may have prompted their tough line. But love toward others does not define too narrow a circle of discipleship. Luke 11:23, which appears contradictory, is the standard we apply to ourselves.

There is victory over racial bigotry (51–56). The One who could pray for his enemies (23:34) could forgive the slight of these Samaritans. Later, in Philip's campaign, Samaria *received* Christ joyfully (Acts 8:4–8).

We are challenged to total discipleship (57–62). The first man (57–58) spoke perfect-sounding words but had never counted the cost of following Jesus. Jesus led a simple life in which material values were held lightly. Do we? The second man looked for a more convenient time. The third man had divided loyalties and, like the lukewarm Laodiceans (Rev. 3:15–16), would always have been looking back wistfully.

My Response

Memory Point

Look up Luke 14:27, and copy this new Key Verse on a 3x5 card. How does this verse apply to today's study?

☐ PRAY to apply God's Word

Lord, my concerns are so often like those of the disciples—self-centered and inappropriate. Help me to see what true greatness is in your sight, and keep me looking ahead, following you.

33

☐ **PRAY for insight into God's Word**
Dear Father, as I study your Word from day to day, show me the concerns of your heart that I may have the same concerns.

☐ **READ Luke 10:1-16**

☐ **MEDITATE on God's Word**

Discovery
1. Why did Jesus send out this large group of missionaries (2)? How did he tell them (and us) to pray?

2. What could they expect on their mission (3)? What was to be their message? Their resources?

3. What details in Jesus' instructions showed his sense of urgency about the mission?

4. In verses 13-15, Jesus grieved for cities that had not responded to his teaching and healing. If you look at a map, you will note that Tyre and Sidon are Gentile cities. What was Jesus saying? What authority did Jesus give to those who went out in his name (16)?

Reflection

Luke alone records the mission of the seventy-two, a reminder that in the Gospels we have only a selection of Jesus' activities from those three packed years. As well as the Twelve, there was this wider fellowship.

The seventy-two, like John the Baptist, shared a ministry of preparation (1). By our testimony we can help predispose people to receive the Lord also. It is surprising, but significant, that Christ's first instruction was to pray for reinforcements (2). Those engaged in the Lord's work know the immensity of the challenge and the inadequacy of the resources. The seventy-two were to travel lightly (4), for simplicity would increase mobility and sense of urgency.

Two scenarios are pictured. *The open door* (5–9) was to be entered without embarrassment or hesitation—two vital attitudes when accepting hospitality. *The closed door* (10–16) was to be recognized as rejection of Christ himself. Instead of continuing to coexist in a kind of uneasy compromise, this rejection and the resulting condemnation were to be made clear.

My Response

Memory Point
Repeat Key Verse 4 (Luke 14:27) twice as you begin to commit it to memory.

☐ PRAY to apply God's Word
Lord, so many people need to hear your Word and to believe in you. I pray you will send workers for the harvest. Help me to be responsible to share the Good News as you use me in the lives of others . . .

34

☐ **PRAY for insight into God's Word**
Father, by the help of your Holy Spirit, help me to see the conflict that takes place in the world from heaven's point of view.

☐ **READ Luke 10:17-24**

☐ **MEDITATE on God's Word**

Discovery
1. How successful was the mission? How did Jesus evaluate it (18)? Do you think the people in the towns along the way understood this great battle between evil and good?

2. What warning did Jesus give the missioners (20)? Why? (See Revelation 3:5.)

3. What made Jesus so full of joy (21-22)? What do you think keeps "learned" people from believing in Jesus?

4. What great privilege was given to Jesus' disciples? Has this privilege been given to you?

Reflection

The mission of the seventy-two disciples was important, and the time of reporting back to Jesus must have been exhilarating for them.

The disciples' joy (17–20). The disciples discovered that by "the power at work within them," they were "able to do far more abundantly" than their original commission (9). Perhaps they should not have been surprised, since they represented, as we do, One who is almighty. He saw a dimension that exceeded their exultation, a victory not over disease and demons only, but over the archenemy, Satan (18). And yet, immediately he added a further dimension for rejoicing (20)—the wonder of heavenly citizenship. Our relationship to God through Christ eclipses every other miracle.

The Savior's joy (21–24). It may have been less than flattering to the disciples to be described as "children," but the New Testament consistently contrasts the childlike (not childish) attitude of responsive trust with the superior attitude of those who, thinking they know, confine their understanding to a mundane, human level. The truth is that we all need a spirit of wisdom and of revelation. Another misconception is imagining that Christ is but one of many ways to God. He is, in fact, *unique,* and it does matter what, or rather *who* we believe. There is only *one way* (John 14:6), *one name* (Acts 4:12), and *one foundation* for our salvation (1 Cor. 3:11).

My Response

Memory Point

Think about the responsibilities of witnessing that Jesus gave to his disciples. What responsibility has he given to you? Review Key Verse 4 (Luke 14:27).

☐ PRAY to apply God's Word

Lord Jesus, thank you for revealing yourself to me that I might believe, and thank you for writing my name in heaven. Help me to feel genuine joy all through this day.

35

☐ **PRAY for insight into God's Word**
"In the morning, O Lord, you hear my voice; in the morning I lay my requests before you and wait in expectation" (Ps. 5:3).

☐ **READ Luke 10:25–42**

☐ **MEDITATE on God's Word**

Discovery
1. What motivated the teacher of the law to question Jesus? How did his own answer condemn him?

2. List the characters in the story Jesus told. What action did each take? Why was the hero in the story such a surprise? (See John 4:9b.)

3. What truth did Jesus make the lawyer face about himself (36–37)? (Notice that Jesus is not so concerned about *who* our neighbor is as about our *being* neighbors and showing mercy.)

4. Imagine yourself in Martha's role. What was her concern? Contrast this with Mary's concern. What truth about herself did Jesus want Martha to face? How do you need to apply the teaching of these two incidents to your own life?

Reflection

How easy it is to state familiar doctrinal truths without actually living them out. Remember that while we can impress others with our orthodoxy, we can't deceive our Lord. Luke shows that Jesus was always aware of *inner* motives. This lawyer was doubtless critical of One who had not graduated through the "usual channels." He was self-opinionated, and put an accent on works—but only within a restricted circle.

The Jews accepted verse 27 as the essence of the Old Testament Law but had virtually confined "neighbor" to their own cozy, all-Jewish club. In Christ's parable, despite the local setting, the barriers rolled away. The gulf of racial bigotry vanished in the light of a man in need. The Samaritan became involved, remaining in the danger area, supplying oil, wine, and bandages (possibly from his own robe). He sacrificed his own comfort and showed continuing concern and financial commitment. Knowing this parable, we cannot restrict "neighbor" to someone we know. With a knowledge of the world peculiar to our generation, we have a responsibility to needy people—worldwide.

Verses 38–42 can be viewed as a footnote to the story of the Good Samaritan. Waiting at the feet of Jesus like Mary allows us to share his mind, to adjust our priorities, and to look compassionately on the whole world.

My Response

Memory Point

Take your 3x5 card with you today as you drive or walk and repeat Key Verse 4 (Luke 14:27) several times, thinking through its practical implications for your life.

☐ PRAY to apply God's Word

Lord, help me to have my priorities right—to be merciful and concerned for others like the Good Samaritan—and to make the best choices in the use of my time and energy . . .

36

☐ **PRAY for insight into God's Word**
"Those who know your name will trust in you" (Ps. 9:10). Help me to understand what this means in a new way today.

☐ **READ Luke 11:1–13**

☐ **MEDITATE on God's Word**

Discovery
1. How does Jesus teach us to address God in prayer? What does calling God *Father* mean to you, especially as you pray?

2. What petitions in this prayer refer to God? What petitions are personal? Are these appropriate to your needs? Can you make this a model for your own prayer life?

3. What point is Jesus making in the humorous parable of verses 5–8? What three verbs should characterize our prayer life before God (9–10)? What promises are given in verse 10?

4. How do we know God is not like the friend who will only answer if we "beat on his door"? (Note the phrase *how much more* in verse 13.)

Reflection

The greatest difficulty experienced by most Christians concerns their prayer life—how can its vitality and the awareness of God's presence be maintained? Most of us have prayed frequently, "Lord, teach us to pray . . ." (1). In answer to this request Christ did three things:

He provided a pattern (2–4). Everything about this prayer is significant. It begins not with the aim of securing something for ourselves, but with God's glory and the concerns of his kingdom. From this vantage point we can pray best for ourselves and for others. In this context of a family looking to a Father, forgiveness received must be accompanied by forgiveness extended (Eph. 4:32; Col. 3:13).

He supplied an illustration (5–8) which teaches the same lesson of perseverance in prayer as Luke 18:1–8. The difference is that God is not like this householder who responded simply to avoid further disruption by his inconsiderate neighbor.

He gave an assurance (9–13). A gracious God delights to answer prayer. The implication is that all lesser gifts are included (Matt. 6:33). We can pray in full confidence. Is this the encouragement we need?

My Response

Memory Point

Review Key Verses 1–4 several times. Talk to someone about the verses you are learning.

☐ PRAY to apply God's Word

Repeat the prayer the Lord taught his disciples . . .

37

☐ PRAY for insight into God's Word

"Call upon me in the day of trouble; I will deliver you, and you will honor me" (Ps. 50:15). Lord, thank you for this open invitation. Now help me as I study today.

☐ READ Luke 11:14–26

☐ MEDITATE on God's Word

Discovery

1. Of what did the people accuse Jesus? (Matthew and Mark identify the accusers as Pharisees and scribes.)

2. How did Jesus refute this accusation (17–18)? How did Jesus claim to drive out demons (20–21)? What was the implication of his ability to do this?

3. Compare verse 23 and verse 17. What principle is Jesus giving here? Apply the principle to your own relationships.

4. What is the point of Jesus' mini-parable in verses 24–26? Why isn't it enough to banish evil from our hearts? What are you doing to make Christ more and more "at home" in your life?

Reflection

Beelzebub (from the Old Testament idol *baal*) was the symbol and personification of evil powers. Three points emerge:

The charge was ridiculous (14–19). These critics were not ignorant men; rather they were the Jerusalem religious authorities. Christ made two points:

—an attack on the forces of evil with the authority of the lord of evil would be a form of self-destruction (17–18);

—the same charge could be leveled against Jewish exorcists (19).

Christ's claim was demonstrable (20–22). Satan's former control was admittedly strong but the Lord had decisively shattered his power.

The condition of Christ's critics was desperate (23–26). In the conflict between Christ and Satan there can be no possible neutrality. These leaders wanted a superficial moral clean-up, but were not concerned about being indwelt by God's dynamic Spirit. Thus they were wide open to repossession by the forces of evil. An empty soul is a dangerous thing. It is not enough to be empty of evil; we must be full of God.

My Response

Memory Point

Write out your own paraphrase of Key Verse 4 (Luke 14:27). What does this verse mean for your life today?

☐ PRAY to apply God's Word

Lord, give me "an undivided heart that I may fear your name" (Ps. 86:11). Take away the divisions in my life that keep me from building something solid, and fill me with the protection of your Holy Spirit . . .

38

☐ PRAY for insight into God's Word
Lord, you are the light of the world. Teach me today to walk in light.

☐ READ Luke 11:27–36

☐ MEDITATE on God's Word

Discovery
1. Verse 27 and 28 are a curious interlude. What is of greater importance than an emotional feeling about motherhood?

2. What was happening in Jesus' public ministry according to verse 29? (See also verse 16.) How did he evaluate the attitude of his hearers?

3. What is the function of light (33)? (See Luke 8:16.)

4. Compare verses 34–36 with the principles found in verses 17 and 23. What do these verses say about mixing evil and good?

Reflection

The paragraphs in today's study seem to be collections of incidents in Jesus' life, which Luke combines in this chapter.

Verses 27–28. Christ insists on the fundamental rather than the incidental—obedience to Jesus is greater than merely a physical relationship to him. (See also Luke 8:21.)

Verses 29–32. Since the way in which Christ will be "the sign of Jonah" (29) to his generation *is still future* (30), the natural interpretation is that, as Jonah was resurrected from virtual death (Jonah 1:17) to preach to Nineveh, so will the risen Christ bring a message of judgment to his unbelieving generation.

Verses 33–36. Ideally, the whole nation of Israel was a "light to the nations" (Isa. 49:6), but the application here is primarily personal. Just as clear sight facilitates the coordinated response of the whole body to its environment, so what men see and hear of Christ should illumine them. If we "switch off" Jesus and refuse to allow him to influence our lives, the result is desperate—darkness (34).

My Response

Memory Point

Put Key Verse 4 (Luke 14:27) in a place where you will see it often today. Repeat it *aloud* each time you see it.

☐ PRAY to apply God's Word

Lord, often you speak to me and I am blind and deaf, like the Pharisees in this passage, completely missing who you are. Then I ask for a sign, for something miraculous to prove your presence. O God, forgive me, and help me to be full of light . . .

39

☐ **PRAY for insight into God's Word**
Lord, help me today to delight in knowing you.

☐ **READ Luke 11:37–54**

☐ **MEDITATE on God's Word**

Discovery
1. The Pharisees had scrupulous ceremonial washing procedures before eating, and here Jesus was criticized for not conforming. What did Jesus say was more important (39–41)?

2. List the other practices of the Pharisees that made Jesus sad. (*Woe* is not so much a calling down of judgment as an expression of regret—*Alas.*)

3. When the lawyers felt insulted, what did Jesus say about their actions and responsibilities (45–52)?

4. How do people today fit the description of these verses? Why do sincere people miss the truth and the knowledge of God?

Reflection

Again the religious authorities of Christ's day closed their eyes to the light. Here Jesus deals ruthlessly with five sins:

Presenting an outward show (39–41). Whenever we do anything merely "to keep up appearances," we come under condemnation and show how insensitive we are to Christ's abiding presence (1 Sam. 16:7).

Being concerned with trivial issues (42). We deceive ourselves easily into thinking that if we show meticulous concern with minor issues, then the major items must necessarily be right. Can you think of matters within your life or fellowship which may reveal this tendency?

Living for recognition (43). A desire for praise is natural to our "old self" (Rom. 6:6); but the *restored person* follows the pattern of Jesus—"gentle and humble in heart" (Matt. 11:29), receiving his commendation from the Father.

Laying down rules from which we excuse ourselves (46). A "don't do what I do, but what I tell you" attitude is not acceptable to Christ. He asks for our integrity and consistency (28).

Debasing the standard (52). By bad example, by inadequate or dishonest teaching, or by watering down the Word of God to please others we become stumbling blocks and fall under special condemnation (Matt. 18:6).

My Response

Memory Point

Review Luke 14:27 again. In light of today's study, why is such radical discipleship important?

☐ PRAY to apply God's Word

Lord, how easy it is to sin by majoring on minor points and thus forgetting what is most important. Clarify my own values today, I pray . . .

40

☐ **PRAY for insight into God's Word**

Open my eyes, Lord, to behold wonderful things from your Word. Help me to apply the warning and teaching of today's passage to my life.

☐ **READ Luke 12:1-12**

☐ **MEDITATE on God's Word**

Discovery

1. Notice who was present and to whom Jesus gave this series of teachings. Then look through the passage and list the four or five basic subjects Jesus covered.

2. Why is hypocrisy a short-sighted way to live (2–3)?

3. Who is the only one worth fearing (4–5)? What do verses 6 and 7 tell you about the way this One cares for you? Do you believe this?

4. What basic loyalty is required of a Christian (8–10)? How does the Holy Spirit help believers (11–12)?

Reflection

The crowds are so great that the people are trampling on each other. It seems like a heady moment for the disciples. Instead Jesus gives them important warnings.

The short-sightedness of hypocrisy (1–3). The hypocrite may have some trifling success in deceiving others, but he cannot deceive God. In the sharpening tension of Christ's relationship with the authorities, *he was the Light* that had revealed the sordid, insidious effects of their hypocrisy. On the final day of judgment that exposure would be consummated. For the Christian the course is clear: we must live in the light (1 John 1:5–7) where deceit is ruled out.

The right kind of fear (4–7). Fear of man can dictate our response, but it cannot go beyond death. God's power to intervene decisively is eternal. Many of the church's martyrs have experienced the assurance of the Father's tender, watchful care noted in verses 6–7. For the believer, fear of God is a wholesome and loving respect—not a cringing terror.

The ultimate standard (8–12). Christ insists that a person's eternal destiny depends on belief and open confession of him. The seriousness of rejecting the Holy Spirit's convicting work and testimony to the Savior (John 16:8–15) is apparent; it is *the unpardoned sin* because it rejects the very ground of salvation. But again Christ quickly balances the picture (11–12): For his followers, the Holy Spirit is not Prosecutor—but Advocate, Teacher, and Comforter.

My Response

Memory Point

Review Luke 14:27 again. How does this kind of discipleship keep one from hypocrisy?

☐ PRAY to apply God's Word

Father God, thank you for knowing all about me and for being concerned for me. Help me to be genuine and honest about my relationship with you . . .

41

☐ **PRAY for insight into God's Word**
Lord, I come before you today as your needy child. Speak to me and fill my heart with your thoughts.

☐ **READ Luke 12:13–34**

☐ **MEDITATE on God's Word**

Discovery
1. How did Jesus happen to tell the story of verses 16–20? What was Jesus warning us about in this incident?

2. Notice the repetition of the words *I* and *my* in the parable of the rich man. Compare this with verse 21. When does a greedy person have enough?

3. Why is worry an inappropriate habit for one who trusts God? How are a person's real values revealed?

4. What makes the "good life" according to today's passage?

Reflection

Along with the warnings of the last study, Jesus gives his disciples some answers to questions that are basic for daily living.

Is Christ disinterested in our everyday affairs (13–15)? A superficial understanding of verse 14 might suggest this, but the Gospels reveal how vitally our Lord was concerned with every aspect of life. The warning about covetousness (15) is so applicable to our generation whose philosophy of life is almost exactly as described. It forms a perilous rat-race into which Christians can easily be drawn.

Are perseverance, diligence, and thoughtfulness to be condemned (16–21)? Again Scripture, especially in books like Proverbs, gives an overwhelming "No!" But look again at the complete self-centeredness of the farmer (17–19). This obsessive preoccupation, with no thought for the future and no concern for the poor, is unbalanced. The words "This very night . . ." dramatically dispel such delusions. But if we have a continuing sense of accountability to God, that "night," whenever it comes, will not catch us unprepared (John 9:4).

Shouldn't we be concerned with basic material needs (22–31)? Yes, but gnawing anxiety about "tomorrow" reveals a basic lack of faith. God knows our need (30). "Give us *each day* our daily bread" (11:3) shows the proper balance between acknowledging need and trusting God to provide. The greatest goal for the Christian, however, is to "seek his kingdom" (31). This involves our personal quest for God himself, his rule in our hearts, and our active participaton in the extension of his kingdom.

My Response

Memory Point

How does Key Verse 4 (Luke 14:27) apply to today's study? Repeat it aloud twice.

☐ PRAY to apply God's Word

O Lord Jesus, help me to see what really makes life good and rich. Make me more and more concerned about treasures in heaven, and keep me from worrying. I believe my Father knows what I need . . .

42

☐ **PRAY for insight into God's Word**

Lord, because I have made you my Lord, I am your servant. Teach me what that means in practical ways, so that I may be faithful.

☐ **READ Luke 12:35–48**

☐ **MEDITATE on God's Word**

Discovery

1. In obvious contrast to worrying about life (yesterday's reading) what concerns should Jesus' disciples have? What attitudes should characterize their lives?

2. What pleasure does such "watchfulness" give the master in Jesus' story? How will he show his pleasure (37)?

3. How did Jesus answer the question Peter asked in verse 41? Who is the diligent servant?

4. Read the last part of verse 48. Note that it is part of the answer to Peter's question. What does it say to you about your own life?

Reflection

After his reassurance about the Father's provision and care, Jesus warns his disciples to be ready and watchful for his return.

Readiness and its reward (35–40). Mention of the kingdom (31–32) involves an attitude of expectant hope aptly described in terms of returning from a marriage feast. The terms "dressed . . . lamps burning . . . waiting" are reminders that being ready for Christ's return involves an inward and an outward preparation—an *attitude* and an *activity*. Have you ever appreciated the joy your faithfulness gives your Master? If not, read verse 37. Note, too, that he is fully aware of those times when maintaining our watchfulness is most difficult (38).

Responsibility and accountability are in direct proportion (41–48). Peter's question required a qualified answer. There is no closed shop in Christ's service. Anyone may enlist and be given a degree of responsibility. Stewards of any rank who lose the expectant hope of their Lord's return can abuse their trust. The features of this abuse are significant (45): *misuse of power, exploitation of others,* and *indulgence of self.* Since Peter and the disciples were certainly included in the scope of this parable, we, too, must guard against failing our Master. Obviously Peter himself took Christ's words to heart (see 1 Peter 1:13).

My Response

Memory Point

Key Verse 4 (Luke 14:27) underscores the teaching of today's study. Say it aloud from memory.

☐ PRAY to apply God's Word

Lord Jesus, by the working of your Holy Spirit make me a faithful and wise servant. I thank you for all you have given me. Help me to be a good steward, for your name's sake . . .

43

☐ **PRAY for insight into God's Word**
Enliven my spirit, Lord, as I read your Word, and give me an understanding heart.

☐ **READ Luke 12:49–59**

☐ **MEDITATE on God's Word**

Discovery
1. How did Jesus speak of his coming ordeal on the cross? What would be its result? What did fire symbolize?

2. In what sense did Jesus come to bring peace, and in what way is his message divisive?

3. In verse 54 Jesus refers to the crowd's demand for a sign. Of what did he accuse them?

4. How did Jesus urge them to repentance (57–59)? In what sense does every person have a case that needs settling before God?

Reflection

Jesus always has the big picture in mind when he speaks. He sees the issues clearly—and beyond the issues into eternity.

A divisive dynamic (49–53). Christ's own ministry is expressed in terms of fire (49). The preceding verses might suggest the fire of judgment (1 Cor. 3:12–15). The immediate context (50), Christ anticipating his ordeal of suffering and longing for its fulfillment, indicates instead the fire of a new, dynamic faith. Compare the zeal of the Spirit-filled disciples, accompanied by tongues of fire (Acts 2:3). This is revolutionary. It disrupts (51–53). No one can be uninvolved over so great an issue; ultimately there is one fundamental division—those who *receive* Christ and those who *reject* Him.

"Seek the Lord while he may be found" (Isa. 55:6). Christ condemns not only the religious authorities but also the multitudes for their moral and spiritual insensitivity (54–59). Excellent weather prophets they might have been, but they lacked any perception about events in their midst. The "present time" for them was the long anticipated moment of their Messiah's coming, yet they were blind to it. Their sin would be plainly revealed and punished. Jesus' illustration was an urgent appeal to repentance, to get right with the Judge.

My Response

Memory Point

Review the four Key Verses you have studied this far in Luke.

☐ PRAY to apply God's Word

Pray for someone you know who has not accepted Jesus Christ as Savior.

44

☐ **PRAY for insight into God's Word**

Open my eyes, Lord . . . I want to see Jesus. Help me to have new insights into who you are today.

☐ **READ Luke 13:1-17**

☐ **MEDITATE on God's Word**

Discovery

1. How did Jesus press home the fact that all people are sinful (1–5)?

2. What does the parable in verses 6–8 show about the mercy of a God who waits for people to repent? How do you define repentance?

3. What was Jesus doing in the synagogue when he noticed the bent-over woman? How was her healing a visual illustration of repentance?

4. Contrast the attitude of the ruler of the synagogue with the attitude of Jesus about the healing of this woman.

Traveling toward Jerusalem/Luke 9:46–19:27

Reflection

Chapters 13 and 14 focus attention on the kingdom of God, which is open to all, but only on certain conditions.

A change is needed in everyone (1–5). Repentance is a primary condition. Jesus will not allow his hearers to accuse either the Galilean zealots (1–2) or the builders of Jerusalem (4) of any greater sin than that which they themselves have committed—all people need to repent or they will perish also (5).

A change is needed now (6–9). The gardener gave the unproductive fig tree one last chance to bear fruit. Jesus tells this parable to illustrate that his listeners are being given one last chance and should make an immediate response to his call for repentance.

A change is gloriously possible (10–17). When Jesus cures the deformed woman, the synagogue ruler is so rigid in his thinking that he objects to this healing because it took place on the Sabbath. Jesus points out how hypocritical he is, for the Law makes provision even for the care of animals on the Sabbath.

My Response

Memory Point

As you repeat Key Verse 4, Luke 14:27, meditate on what it means to carry your cross and follow Jesus.

☐ **PRAY to apply God's Word**

Lord, make me open to being changed by you. Show me any area in my life where repentance is overdue . . .

45

☐ PRAY for insight into God's Word

Father, I come before you today with a heart already full of other thoughts and concerns. Help me to see basic truths in your Word today so that I may strip away the unimportant in my life.

☐ READ Luke 13:18–35

☐ MEDITATE on God's Word

Discovery

1. What do you learn about the kingdom of God from the two parables in verses 18–20? Compare your answers with your personal experience of the kingdom of God.

2. Why did Jesus give such a grim picture about salvation in verses 22–30? In a few words, write what you understand him to be saying in answer to the question of verse 23.

3. What is the difference between those who knock on the closed door (25) and those who will take their places at the feast (29)? Notice the claims of the first group (26).

4. What do you see of Jesus' purposefulness, compassion, and trust in God's sovereignty in verses 31–35? How can we have these same attitudes?

Reflection

The kingdom of God doesn't follow the rules of this world's system—which emphasize being big and powerful, having the right connections, and worrying about personal safety. Everything about the kingdom of God is different. The two parables that open today's reading illustrate the kingdom's outward growth (18–19) and inward power (20–21).

If a person is to enter it, then he or she must repent and enter this narrow door by Christ alone, rather than rely on moral achievements. Jesus illustrates his message with the householder who will not open the closed door to those who merely have a superficial acquaintance (26) with him and no personal knowledge (27). Many Gentiles, who were called last, would enter the kingdom before privileged Jews who were not relying on Christ alone.

The rebellious rulers—and King Herod too—would hate this teaching (Luke 3:19–20). But Jesus is not threatened by Herod's disapproval. His life is in the hands of a sovereign Father, not an ungodly king (32).

Christ knows that, like so many prophets before him, he must die in Jerusalem. He has made every attempt to win his contemporaries, but without widespread success. Like their ancestors, they hurl stones in the face of love.

My Response

Memory Point

Review Key Verse 4 (Luke 14:27) from your 3x5 card. Notice again how it speaks to the passage you have just studied. Say the verse aloud three times, checking to see how well you have memorized it.

☐ PRAY to apply God's Word

Lord, what a terrible thing it is to be *unwilling* in relation to the living God. Make me eager to be gathered to your side to be comforted, sustained, and taught, for Jesus' sake . . .

46

☐ **PRAY for insight into God's Word**
Lord Jesus, help me to be a willing disciple and to put into practice whatever you show me, for my own good and your glory . . .

☐ **READ Luke 14:1–11**

☐ **MEDITATE on God's Word**

Discovery
1. What was the atmosphere surrounding the hospitality given to Jesus at the home of this prominent Pharisee?

2. What was Jesus' motive in asking the Pharisee and the other experts on the law the two questions of verses 3 and 5? What did they say about themselves by their refusal to answer Jesus' questions?

3. What motivated Jesus to tell the parable of verses 8–10, and what is the point of the story?

4. Put in your own words what Jesus is teaching you from the two incidents in today's reading.

Reflection

If we imagine that it is only *what* we do that matters, and that *why* we do it is unimportant, today's reading should disillusion us—fast!

Motives matter more than tradition (1–6). Those sharp-eyed lawyers and Pharisees (3) were always, it seems, anxious to trap Jesus. The keeping of the Sabbath was obviously a burning issue with them. So Jesus faced them with their own question (3)! No wonder they couldn't answer (4)—especially when he turned the question to refer to their own animals. If it was right to rescue beasts on the Sabbath—why not people? It's worth asking how many of our actions and attitudes are motivated by prejudice, convenience, tradition, truth, or love.

Motives matter more than prestige (7–11). Maybe, at the time, it seems important to claim a place at the table appropriate to our status. (Or rather, what we think our status ought to be!) But it becomes desperately humiliating if our host thinks differently about us (9). On the other hand, if we're not "thinking ourselves big," our host may respect our humility and "exalt" us (11). This is true in the realm of social courtesy—but even more true when we are the guests, and the host is God. It's what God thinks of us that matters.

My Response

Memory Point

Use your four memory cards to review the Key Verses you have learned from Luke's gospel (Luke 1:37; 3:6; 5:31–32; 14:27). Can you say them from memory, giving the references for each one?

☐ PRAY to apply God's Word

Lord, forgive me for thinking more highly of myself than I ought. Keep me from the kind of fuzzy thinking that makes outward forms more valuable than any of the people who touch my life . . .

47

☐ **PRAY for insight into God's Word**
Lord Jesus, you take the common events of everyday to teach spiritual lessons. Do that for me today, Lord, and help me to make the right application in my personal life.

☐ **READ Luke 14:12–24**

☐ **MEDITATE on God's Word**

Discovery
1. What motivates people to give a party?

2. What kind of party-giving did Jesus recommend, and what are its rewards?

3. In the story Jesus told (16–23), why were some invitations to the banquet refused? Who was willing to accept the invitation?

4. Who is the "certain man" of the story in verse 16? Why do people refuse God's invitation today? What is your response to his invitation?

Reflection

In the last reading, the motives of a guest at a dinner party were highlighted—emphasizing particularly the danger of self-importance. In today's reading, a dinner or banquet is still the Lord's aid for teaching about the kingdom of God.

Not by works. The Pharisees performed their good works for God in the belief that he in turn would repay them with kindness and benevolent favor. It was like asking wealthy people to a meal so that they in turn would invite you to their luxurious table (12). But God does not act like that. He gives abundantly to those who cannot hope to repay him. Those who love God should give generously (13) without thought of repayment. God promises to bless such generosity.

"Everything is now ready." The banquet imagery is retained in Christ's unforgettable parable of the insolent guests who had accepted the initial invitation (16) to the banquet, but when the messengers came to inform the guests that the meal was about to be served (17), made ridiculous excuses and did not come.

The prophets had issued the invitation in Old Testament times and traditionally at least, Israel had responded—but not in sincerity. Now Christ had come and the banquet was ready, but the Jews would not believe (John 1:11). The invitation would now be extended to the Gentiles.

My Response

Memory Point

Be sure to put Key Verse 4 (Luke 14:27) where you can remember to repeat it at least twice a day.

☐ PRAY to apply God's Word

Heavenly Father, thank you that you want your house filled and that your invitation includes me. Keep me from being an excuse-maker when you ask anything of me . .

48

☐ **PRAY for insight into God's Word**
Lord Jesus, teach me new truths today about being part of your kingdom. Make the Key Verse more than something I say with my lips—make it the response of my heart.

☐ **READ Luke 14:25–35**

☐ **MEDITATE on God's Word**

Discovery
1. Put the requirements Jesus makes for disciples (26–27) in your own words.

Note: When a Jew of Bible times wanted to say he "preferred" one thing to another, he expressed it as "hating" one and "loving" the other—an example of Oriental hyperbole.

2. What do the two illustrations (28 and 31) tell about the patience, perseverance, and realistic assessment necessary to be a disciple? What does the illustration of salt (34) add to the demands of being a disciple?

3. Review again the purposefulness of Jesus' life by turning back to Luke 9:21–25 and 51. What did Jesus face in Jerusalem?

4. In light of that, how do you respond to his strong words in verse 33 of today's reading?

Reflection

In today's reading, any idea from the earlier banquet picture that the Christian life represents "a soft option" is firmly dispelled. Christ's would-be disciples must know that there will be a cost in family life and a cost in resources.

Costly commitment (25–27). The crowds were eager to follow Jesus when they imagined that all they had to do was sit as his guests at the coming messianic feast (25), but he pointed out that total loyalty to him might result in the loss of one's closest relations (26), and certainly in the loss of one's own independence (27).

Intelligent commitment (28–33). Those who follow him must not be swept along like the crowd (25), moved to make a merely emotional response (9:57–58). Counting the cost is essential.

Effective commitment (34–35). This sacrificial kind of living is not simply a matter between ourselves and Christ; it affects others. Jesus' salt illustration suggests a believer's refining and purifying influence in the community.

My Response

Memory Point

Key Verse 4 (Luke 14:27) should speak powerfully to you in today's study. Repeat it aloud, and then use it as part of your prayer.

☐ PRAY to apply God's Word

Show me, Holy Spirit, where my loyalties are divided between Jesus and other things. Help me to count the cost of discipleship and to follow you gladly . . .

49

☐ **PRAY for insight into God's Word**

Open my eyes, Lord, I want to see Jesus. Make yourself and your love real to me today.

☐ **READ Luke 15:1-10**

☐ **MEDITATE on God's Word**

Discovery

1. Why did Jesus tell these parables (1-2)?

2. In these two parables (3 and 8) who took the initiative to find what was lost? Who do these seekers represent?

3. What observations do you make about the diligence of the seeker in each case? What did the seeker do when he found the lost?

4. How did Jesus apply these two parables to show the critical Pharisees what God is like (7, 10)? Have the angels had a celebration in heaven over you?

Reflection

It was intended as sneering, bitter criticism—Christ received sinners and ate with them (2). But possibly no other verse so perfectly defines our Lord's attitude. He did receive sinners, and they responded to him. His challenging words about the *cost* of discipleship (Luke 14) stirred something in them. His genuine love and care contrasted with a cold, conventional religion, so blatantly indifferent to the fate of the lost. These incomparable parables stress three points:

Ownership. To be lost implies ownership. The sheep and the coin had owners, and tax collectors and sinners belonged to God. Remember that while our Lord accepts the Pharisees' estimate of themselves (7), *all* men are lost, even the most eminently religious (Rom 3:9–19).

Sacrificial compassion. God's nature is revealed in the strenuous sacrificial search (4, 8). Notice our Lord's assumption of deity here; the imagery, in each case, speaks of his mission (see Luke 19:10).

Restoration. When the divine heart is satisfied by the restoration of the lost, the heavenly host rejoices! This joy *ought* to have echoed and re-echoed in the hearts of the Pharisees—sadly, it did not!

To be "found" by Christ is surely the most joyous experience in the world. While they were lost, the sheep and the coin were useless. To be "found" is to know that you are saved, secure, and usable.

My Response

Memory Point

Today would be a good setting for repeating Key Verse 3 (Luke 5:31–32) from memory. Then repeat Luke 14:27. How do these two verses emphasize God's grace and our responsibility?

☐ PRAY to apply God's Word

Thank you, heavenly Father, that you looked for me, found me, and that you keep on patiently working with me. Thank you that you are still seeking the lost . . .

50

☐ **PRAY for insight into God's Word**
Thank you, Father God, for your consistency and diligence in reaching me and receiving me. Thank you for being the kind of heavenly Father I need.

☐ **READ Luke 15:11–32**

☐ **MEDITATE on God's Word**

Discovery

1. Write down the words or phrases that outline the story of the son's desire to live independently of the father. What happened to bring the young man to his senses?

2. What evidence do you find of genuine repentance in the younger son?

3. What observations do you make about the father's love for the son? Contrast the elder son. Was he enjoying the father's fellowship while serving him?

4. Apply the parable. What is Jesus teaching you about your heavenly Father in his relationship to both kinds of sons? What is always cause for rejoicing?

Reflection

How perfectly this story reveals the hearts of sinful people and the loving, outreaching heart of God the Father! Consider briefly the key phrases:

"Give me" (12). Here is evidence of humankind's grasping, self-centered rebellious will. *"A distant country"* (13). It was, in fact, near enough for an easy return home for the half-starved youth (20). Alienation from God, however, is not measured in distance, but in attitude. *"He squandered"* (13). When self is in control, one's gifts and possessions are inevitably prostituted.

"He began to be in need" (14). The sharp pressure of adversity revealed to the now friendless prodigal his bankruptcy, which was moral and spiritual as well as material. *"I will go back . . . I have sinned . . . I am no longer worthy"* (18–19). In this carefully rehearsed speech there was no particularly high motive, just an acute sense of need. But the God of grace responds readily to the slightest sign of genuine repentance.

"His father saw him" (20). Even this sublime description fails to parallel the initiative of the gracious heavenly Father, who seeks out the prodigal in the far country. This was the mission of Christ. The son's return was an occasion for rejoicing—the pharisaic attitude of the older brother was repellent (28–32).

My Response

Memory Point

Review all of the Key Verses from your study in Luke this far. Note their relevance to today's study.

☐ PRAY to apply God's Word

Father, thank you for your loving, forgiving heart. Keep me from being like either son in the story today. Help me comprehend what you mean when you say "everything I have is yours" (31) . . .

51

☐ PRAY for insight into God's Word

Speak, Lord, for your servant is listening. Give me ears to hear and a heart to obey whatever you want to say to me, for my good and for your glory.

☐ READ Luke 16:1-18

☐ MEDITATE on God's Word

Discovery

1. This seems a strange story for Jesus to tell. For what did the master in the story commend the steward? Nevertheless, how is the steward described in verse 8? What is the difference between saying, "I commend this steward because he acted shrewdly," and "I commend this steward because he acted dishonestly"?

2. What point about the use of money did Jesus make from the parable (8b and 9)?

3. What larger principle of stewardship is found in verses 10–13? What do you learn about the importance of being *whole-hearted* in what you value?

4. Of what did Jesus accuse the Pharisees? Realizing that *God knows your heart* can be either a source of comfort or discomfort. What makes the difference?

Note: The Pharisees used their laws to cover up their sins, hence Jesus' words in verse 15. Jesus underscores the importance of the law of God (17) and in particular mentions one area (18) that was hotly debated by the various groups of religious leaders.

Reflection

The "parable of the clever rascal" (1–9) must not be treated as an allegory. We should look for the central point in the story and not try to relate every detail to a different aspect of truth. The key truth is in verse 8b. Even godless people are smart enough to use the resources given to them. The estate manager realized he was in trouble, so he acted generously toward his master's debtors, hoping that in the months ahead, they would remember his crafty kindness!

Jesus is not commending his theft—the man is described as "dishonest." But he illustrates *the believer's need for astuteness, initiative, and ingenuity.* The dishonest steward was wise enough to make his present opportunities serve his future welfare (8–9).

The money-loving Pharisees (14) foolishly believed that material possessions were a sure sign of God's approval. Jesus insisted that prosperity, in itself, indicates nothing. It is what a man does with it that is important. Our attitude toward money is a crucial test of our devotion to God (13).

My Response

Memory Point

Recite Key Verse 4 (Luke 14:27) from memory. Note its emphasis on whole-heartedness.

☐ PRAY to apply God's Word

Lord Jesus, help me to be a wise and faithful steward of all you've entrusted to me. Show me areas in my life where I lack whole-heartedness in my commitment to you . . .

52

☐ **PRAY for insight into God's Word**
Lord Jesus, thank you for telling stories to reveal eternal truths and for teaching me in ways I cannot ignore. I come before you again today, open to what you want me to see about yourself and your values.

☐ **READ Luke 16:19–31**

☐ **MEDITATE on God's Word**

Discovery
1. Contrast the life-style of both the rich man and of Lazarus on earth.

Note: Lazarus is the only character in the parables with a name, and his name, which means God is my helper, *is a clue to his spiritual condition.*

2. Contrast the situations of the two after death.

3. The Jewish leaders taught that riches were a sign of blessing and acceptance from God. How would the details of this story have affected the Pharisees who listened (14)?

4. What two requests did the rich man make? Ponder Abraham's answer about Moses and the prophets (29, 31). Remember who told this story. Was Abraham's comment in verse 31 accurate?

Reflection

One Bible commentator has called this central section of Luke "The Gospel of the Outcasts." Several of the parables Jesus tells in these chapters focus on the unwanted people in society.

In 14:13, for example, we are told to invite the poor, the crippled, and the blind when we give a dinner. In 14:21, the servants go out into the streets and alleys of the town to bring the disadvantaged to the great banquet. In 15:22 a wasteful, prodigal son is welcomed back home.

Today's parable must have shocked its hearers. How slow the Jewish leaders were to understand that the kingdom of heaven has different values from their own. In this story the Pharisees learn that the rich man's wealth was no indication of his piety. He was cast into hell (Hades) tormented and full of remorse, whereas the beggar was carried to Abraham's bosom. *It is not what you possess that matters; it is what you do with it.* This does not mean that salvation is gained by merit or deeds. But it is a necessary reminder that *the way we behave as Christians in this life is of immense significance to the next* (2 Cor. 5:10).

My Response

Memory Point
Review all of the Key Verses you have learned from Luke's gospel.

☐ **PRAY to apply God's Word**
Lord, this parable gives a powerful picture of heaven and hell. Thank you that personal faith in Jesus brings me from death to life, and that eternal life is a present possession. Help me to listen to Moses and the prophets today—to take seriously the study of your Word.

53

☐ **PRAY for insight into God's Word**

For thy daily mercies, be Thy named adored,
More than all, I thank Thee for Thyself, O Lord.
Frank Houghton

☐ **READ Luke 17:1–19**

☐ **MEDITATE on God's Word**

Discovery

1. Summarize the subjects Jesus discusses in verses 1–10.

2. What attitudes are necessary for a disciple to live out these teachings?

3. What did the ten lepers ask for (11–13)? What was Jesus asking them to do, by telling them to show themselves to the priest? When were the ten men healed (14)?

Note: The priest acted as a health inspector to certify that a cure had taken place.

4. What was Jesus' expectation from these ten men (17–18)? Who remembered to be thankful? How do you think this affected his relationship with Jesus? How long has it been since you thanked God for cleansing you?

Reflection

Here Jesus describes the qualities a disciple needs.

Exemplary conduct (1–2). "No man is an island." Our everyday behavior affects others—for good?

Generous forgiveness (3–4). And what if we are sinned against? There is a place for compassionate rebuke, but the ministry of gracious correction is largely neglected by modern Christians. Jesus "rebuked" his disciples but always with love (Mark 8:33). When a brother or sister genuinely seeks forgiveness, it must never be withheld, no matter how grieved we may be about the sin.

Adventurous faith (5–6). The apostles probably felt they did not have faith rich and resourceful enough for such demands. Jesus urges them to "think big" when they consider what God can do. He can even explode petty human resentments and churlishly unforgiving attitudes.

Devoted service (7–10). Even if we obey God in all these things, there is no room for self-congratulation. It is what we are expected to do. We are at God's disposal, and our role is that of the obedient slave (10).

Adoring gratitude (11–19). The story of the grateful Samaritan has timeless appeal. But it is easy to forget.

My Response

Memory Point

Apply Key Verse 4 (Luke 14:27) to the kind of discipleship Jesus is talking about in today's study. Then repeat the verse aloud.

☐ PRAY to apply God's Word

"Praise the LORD, O my soul, and *forget not all his benefits*" (Ps. 103:2) . . .

54

☐ **PRAY for insight into God's Word**

Make me fully alive and aware, Lord, as I meet with you today. Stamp your way of thinking on my mind so I may become more like you.

☐ **READ Luke 17:20–37**

☐ **MEDITATE on God's Word**

Discovery

1. What do you think the Pharisees had in mind when they asked Jesus about the kingdom of God? What is the secret of the kingdom of God? Compare this passage with Luke 13:18–21.

2. Define what is meant by "the day of the Son of Man." While people were curious about "that day," what did Jesus say must happen first (25)?

3. What examples did Jesus use to warn against a self-centered life-style that ignores the reality of the Lord's return?

4. What principle of life did Jesus re-emphasize here (33)? Compare this with Luke 9:23–24.

Reflection
As in Jesus' time, people today have a great curiosity about the Lord's return to earth and the end of human history. They are not so much interested in commitment to truth as in speculation about the unknown future.

The kingdom within you (20–21). Jesus' answer to the Pharisees contradicted the current popular expectation of a spectacular divine intervention, concerned mainly with material and political aims. The Pharisees looked intently for such a kingdom. But their misconceptions blinded them to the fact that, with the establishment of Christ's kingly rule in the hearts of men, God's kingdom was already established.

The coming kingdom (22–37). There will be, however, a final and dramatic intervention when God's kingdom will be consummated. Until then, Jesus predicted many difficult days for his disciples, when the very intensity of desire for Christ's return would lead to frequent false alarms (22–23).

But Christ's return will be sudden, and its decisive brilliance (24) will preclude further speculation. Tragically, as so often in biblical history (26–29), his coming will burst in on a world preoccupied and complacent in its gross materialism. It may even catch the church unprepared—hence the advice to recognize true values. The man on the rooftop should not worry about the goods in the house (31). Preoccupation with such things is to recall the fate of Lot's wife (32) who looked to the things that were seen rather than the unseen truth of God's plan for ultimate salvation.

My Response

Memory Point
Obviously the kind of discipleship that Key Verse 4 (Luke 14:27) prescribes is important from first to last. Repeat the verse from memory.

☐ PRAY to apply God's Word
Lord, how clear it is from this passage that salvation is a personal matter. Help me to live in such a way that I will be ready for your return at any time . . .

55

☐ **PRAY for insight into God's Word**
Lord, I do need to be taught how to pray and to believe that it matters *that I do* pray. Help me to a new level of understanding and commitment as I study today.

☐ **READ Luke 18:1–14**

☐ **MEDITATE on God's Word**

Discovery
1. Why did Jesus tell the story of the unjust judge and the widow (1)?

2. What was commendable about the widow? What was uncommendable about the judge?

3. What sharp contrast exists between God and the judge, both in their view of the supplicants and in their desire to answer the requests?

4. Why did Jesus tell the story beginning in verse 9? What principle about prayer is clear from this parable (14)?

Reflection
Don't give up, Jesus says. Pray. And then he teaches us the attitudes that make prayer meaningful.

Pray with expectancy (1–8). The poverty-stricken widow was utterly helpless and could only obtain her desire by constant and relentless pressure. She refused to give up. She kept coming back (3). The phrase "wear me out" (5) literally means "give me a black eye!" If the apathetic judge, who felt no moral constraints to deal justly, responded to her persistent appeal, how much more, Jesus suggests, will our loving and caring Father willingly meet our deeply-felt needs? God's elect people, who cry to him "day and night," can expect a speedier, more equitable answer (7) than that given by the heartless judge. Yet how soon our patience is exhausted, how easily we give up praying if we do not receive an immediate answer from God. That is why Jesus commends to us a faith that persists (8).

Pray in humility (9–14). The second parable has the spiritually unprepared Pharisees clearly in view. At his coming, the Son of Man will certainly not "find faith" (8) in such self-reliant people, more concerned about other people's moral failures (11) and their own religious achievements (12) than in their personal unworthiness (13a) and God's abundant mercy (13b). The man who goes to God's house boastfully will return to his own house despondently.

My Response

Memory Point
Take out your 3x5 cards and review all the Key Verses you have learned from Luke's gospel. How many can you say from memory?

☐ PRAY to apply God's Word
Pray for someone you have "given up on," and keep praying for that person.

56

☐ **PRAY for insight into God's Word**
Lord Jesus, show me the difference between being child-like and being childish in my relationship with you. Give me a trusting, obedient heart, for your name's sake.

☐ **READ Luke 18:15–30**

☐ **MEDITATE on God's Word**

Discovery
1. Contrast the attitude of the disciples toward the children with Jesus' actions toward them. How does a child receive the kingdom of God?

2. What kind of man was the ruler of verse 18? What was he concerned about? What was the caliber of his character and life?

3. Why did the ruler go away saddened? Why is it difficult for those who are rich to enter the kingdom of God? How does this story penetrate to the heart of what is required to enter the kingdom of God?

4. What is the reward of those who practice the kind of discipleship Jesus asks for (29–30)?

Reflection

The three great interrelated themes in today's reading impress upon us the price of true Christian discipleship.

Dependence (15–17). Busy and preoccupied, the disciples were indignant at the intrusion of these parents. Jesus explained that in seeking his blessing these parents were depending on his help. The Pharisee in the preceding parable relied on his works; the ruler in the following narrative relied on his wealth. Morals and money are poor substitutes for true faith and child-like dependence on God.

Obedience (18–23). Possibly no other incident demonstrates so clearly the impossibility of earning salvation as does Christ's encounter with this young ruler. He had everything, humanly speaking: possessions, position, and personality. He had also attained a formal righteousness, with a star next to all the commandments dealing with human relationships (20–21). This man was also perceptive, for he was aware that he still lacked eternal life. Christ challenged him to give up material possessions for the life of discipleship (22). This young man, and all who fail to meet Christ's challenge and then draw back, are sad (23).

Commitment (24–30). Riches can easily obstruct a person's entrance to the kingdom (24–25). Peter's assertion that the disciples had done all that the ruler could not do (compare verses 22 and 28) was met by Christ's assurance that all such sacrifices will seem trival compared with God's immense generosity now and his incalculable blessings in eternity.

My Response

Memory Point

How does verse 29 of today's study relate to Key Verse 4 (Luke 14:27)? Repeat the verse from memory.

☐ PRAY to apply God's Word

Show me, Father, anything in my life that I am clinging to at the expense of obedience to you. Help me to give it up . . .

57

☐ **PRAY for insight into God's Word**
Open my eyes, Lord Jesus, to see the needs of those around me and to see you at work in my life today.

☐ **READ Luke 18:31–43**

☐ **MEDITATE on God's Word**

Discovery
1. What details about his death did Jesus share with his disciples (31–33)? Note at least nine details.

2. Why do you think the disciples were so slow to understand what would happen in Jerusalem?

3. Describe the condition of the man by the roadside. Compare the title the crowds gave Jesus with what the blind man called him. What did he seem to believe about Jesus? Does this account for his persistence?

Note: Son of David *is a messianic title.*

4. In contrast to the crowds, notice the dignity with which Jesus treated this man who was a beggar (40–42). How does the blind man's response to Jesus (43) challenge you about your personal response to him?

Reflection

Today's reading is about two kinds of blindness, intellectual and physical.

The disciples (31–34). Peter had just mentioned the sacrifice of the disciples (28), but Jesus took them aside and told them of the greater sacrifice he would make. Noting how frequently our Lord spoke about his future suffering, we marvel at the disciples' dullness of comprehension. They were thoroughly conditioned to the expectation of a conquering Davidic Messiah, not a Suffering Servant.

We all have an inbuilt capacity to be selective in examining evidence, to reject what does not fit our preconceived ideas. For example, many Christians balk at the warnings of hardship involved in discipleship, although Jesus makes his terms perfectly plain (9:23–25). Once aware of this tendency, we can learn, as Christ insisted, to count the cost of following him (14:27–33).

The blind man (35–43).

—He knew his condition only too well, with its shame and dull routine.

—When Christ approached, he did not allow discouragement to keep him from the one who could surely help (39).

—He was specific about his fundamental need (41); had he merely asked for alms he would soon have returned to his beggar's life.

—The man did not know it, but this was his last opportunity; never again did Christ pass through Jericho. Likewise, people must not expect unlimited opportunities of receiving salvation.

—Finally, note Christ's love and compassion. Traveling to Jerusalem—and a cross—he responded instantly, as always, to the cry of need.

My Response

Memory Point

Repeat Key Verse 4 (Luke 14:27). What does it mean to you to take up your cross daily? (See Luke 9:23–24.)

☐ PRAY to apply God's Word

How would you answer the Lord Jesus' question, "What do you want me to do for you?" Prayer is talking with him. Tell him what you feel you need . . .

58

☐ **PRAY for insight into God's Word**

Lord Jesus, meet my need as you did for those you met along the way when you lived on earth. Have mercy on me, O Lord.

☐ **READ Luke 19:1–10**

☐ **MEDITATE on God's Word**

Discovery

1. Contrast the reputation and life-style of Zacchaeus and the blind man of 18:35–43. Compare their needs.

2. How did the people evaluate both Zacchaeus (7) and the blind man (18:39)? Contrast their response with Jesus' way of meeting deep personal needs, seeing beneath the exterior.

3. What would some of Zacchaeus's deep personal needs have been?

4. What is the evidence that "salvation" came to Zacchaeus's house? To your house?

Reflection

In three successive readings we note Christ's encounters with the rich ruler, the blind man, and Zacchaeus. Although his earthly ministry lasted only three brief years, he always had time for individuals, and he dealt with each one as a person. The dominant motive of his ministry is given in verse 10—to save the lost.

Doubtless Zacchaeus was immensely rich, for Jericho was a wealthy agricultural center, and he was the chief tax collector. Money cannot buy friends, however. Zacchaeus was clearly earnest in his desire to see Jesus—his determination was revealed in his ingenious, if undignified, scheme (4)!

Had he heard that Jesus, at the risk of scandalizing the self-righteous, was the friend of tax collectors (15:1), prostitutes (7:39), and other social outcasts like himself (7)? If so, he was not disappointed, for his spontaneous reaction (6) reveals the warm personal friendliness of the Savior's approach (5). Many religious people lived in Jericho, but Jesus chose to stay with a tax collector—is this instructive for us?

This local tax collector is the second rich man to appear in this section of Luke (see 18:18-23). Both appear to have been covetous, but one was morally upright (18:20-21), the other a blatant thief (8). One came boldly to Christ with his questions; the other sought to see and hear Jesus secretly. Yet where the first went away from Christ (18:23), the other "welcomed him gladly" (6).

My Response

Memory Point

Compare Luke 19:10 with Key Verse 3 (Luke 5:31-32). Repeat it from memory, if you can.

☐ PRAY to apply God's Word

Thank you, Lord, that you are always looking for people who know they are needy. I'm so glad it is safe to come to you with my own bundle of needs and complexities.

59

☐ **PRAY for insight into God's Word**
Challenge me today, dear Lord, in ways that I need for personal growth.

☐ **READ Luke 19:11-27**

☐ **MEDITATE on God's Word**

Discovery
1. Why did Jesus tell this story (11)?

2. What trust did the king place in his servants when he went away? Contrast the servants with the other subjects.

3. When the king returned, on what basis did he reward his servants?

4. What principle of personal responsibility did Jesus apply in this parable?

Traveling toward Jerusalem/Luke 9:46–19:27

Reflection

For some time Luke has been describing a journey to Jerusalem (9:51). Jericho is about seventeen miles from Jerusalem, and the journey is almost over. The people thought that on his arrival Jesus would receive public acclaim and usher in his kingdom. Jesus told a parable to correct these false notions.

The parable tells us four important truths: 1) It clarifies the time of the appearance of the kingdom of God. 2) It realistically portrays the coming rejection, departure, and future return of Jesus. 3) It describes the disciples' role while the Lord is away. 4) It teaches how responsibility and reward are related.

Most of the parable focuses on the faithfulness of the servants. When accounts are settled, rewards are given in proportion to faithfulness. The one servant who did nothing with his trust has his mina (or talent) given to the one who proved he could make good use of it. There is no such thing as standing still in the Christian life. Either we grow or we lose what ground we have gained.

My Response

Memory Point

You have come to the last study of this section of Luke's gospel. Say Key Verse 4 (Luke 14:27) aloud. If you have time, look back over the studies beginning with 9:46 and observe again how much of what you have studied is summarized by this Key Verse.

☐ PRAY to apply God's Word

Lord, I know I have a treasure within me, even though I am only a *clay jar* (2 Cor. 4:7). Help me to use what you have given for your glory . . .

5/Jesus in Jerusalem
Luke 19:28—21:38

☐ Introduction

An ancient legend tells how Nero fiddled while Rome burned. It's a word picture that captures the imagination. We use that phrase to describe someone who misses the point, someone so absorbed with the trivial that he fails to grasp the important.

It's a human failing. We do it all the time. Absorbed with the demands of small duties, we miss the beauty of sunsets—and worse still, the wonder of a small child. We're too busy doing the urgent unimportant to visit our mother, to write that letter, to listen . . . We tend to live toward the future and fail to treasure the present moment until it is gone. Then we look back with regret and say, "If only I had known . . ."

Certainly Jesus' disciples must have felt that way, looking back. Did they grasp the relevance of the triumphal entry into Jerusalem, or were they busy keeping up with the crowd? Did they understand what the religious leaders were doing, or were they worried about being the greatest in the kingdom? Did they listen to what Jesus said? Why didn't they ask more questions?

Maybe it was because they were fussing over the urgent present—seeing the *what,* but not the *why.* Would they have valued their time with Jesus more, used it more wisely, if they had understood he was going to die? Would you have done so?

As you study these passages that describe Jesus' last week with the disciples, picture yourself as one of them. You have the advantage of a backward look. Listen to what Jesus says in these days before he dies as if you had a second chance to live through important events and see the value you missed before.

☐ Key Verse 5: Luke 21:33
Heaven and earth will pass away, but my words will never pass away.

☐ Outline of the Gospel of Luke

I. Birth and Childhood Narratives *1:1–2:52*
  A. John's birth and mission foretold   *1:1–25*
  B. Jesus' birth and mission foretold   *1:26–56*
  C. Zechariah's blessing   *1:57–80*
  D. Jesus' birth   *2:1–40*
  E. The boy Jesus at the temple   *2:41–52*

II. Preparation for the Good News *3:1–4:13*
  A. John the Baptist's ministry   *3:1–14*
  B. Jesus' baptism   *3:15–23*
  C. Jesus' temptation   *4:1–13*

III. Jesus in Galilee *4:14–9:45*
  A. Jesus in Nazareth and Capernaum   *4:14–44*
  B. Jesus' call to faith   *5:1–6:11*
  C. Jesus' call and teaching of the Twelve   *6:12–49*
  D. Jesus' compassion   *7:1–50*
  E. Understanding Jesus' ministry   *8:1–56*
  F. Understanding who Jesus is   *9:1–45*

IV. Traveling toward Jerusalem *9:46–19:27*
  A. Realities of discipleship   *9:46–10:42*
  B. Teaching about prayer   *11:1–13*
  C. Jesus' response to criticism   *11:14–12:12*
  D. Jesus' instructions to his disciples   *12:13–12:59*
  E. Call to repentance and faith   *13:1–35*
  F. Teaching about values   *14:1–16:31*
  G. Forgiveness and faith   *17:1–19*
  H. The coming kingdom   *17:20–18:30*
  I. Jesus nearing Jerusalem   *18:31–19:27*

V. Jesus in Jerusalem *19:28–21:38*
  A. Triumphal entry *19:28–48*
  B. Teaching in the temple area *20:1–21:4*
  C. Signs of the end of the age *21:5–38*

VI. Jesus' Last Hours with His Disciples *22:1–53*
  A. The upper room   *22:1–38*
  B. In the garden   *22:39–53*

VII. Arrest and Crucifixion *22:54–23:56*
  A. Denial and mockery   *22:54–71*
  B. Trial   *23:1–25*
  C. Crucifixion and burial   *23:26–56*

VIII. Resurrection *24:1–53*
  A. Empty tomb   *24:1–12*
  B. Road to Emmaus   *24:13–35*
  C. Joyful disciples   *24:36–53*

60

☐ **PRAY for insight into God's Word**
Stir my heart to joyful praise today. Let me sing hosannas to the King of kings.

☐ **READ Luke 19:28–48**

☐ **MEDITATE on God's Word**

Discovery
1. What were Jesus' preparations for his entry into Jerusalem?

2. What statement did Jesus make about himself by the way he entered the city and the adulation he accepted from the crowds (38, 40)?

3. Why did Jesus weep over Jerusalem? Of what were the people totally unaware (44b)?

4. What words describe Jesus' emotions and actions as he entered Jerusalem and the temple?

Reflection

Jesus' entry into Jerusalem was no sudden, impulsive action. He had set his face toward Jerusalem weeks before. He did not leave preparations until the last minute. *The Lord needs it* was a prearranged password.

What an action of courage and glorious proclamation his entry into the city was! He could have slipped in unseen, knowing he was a man with a price on his head. Instead, he deliberately fulfilled the words of the prophets (see Zechariah 9:9), acting out a kind of parable about his kingship.

Only in war did kings ride horses. When they came in peace, they rode a donkey. Arriving on the foal of a donkey, Christ came as a king of love and peace, with one last invitation to the people. If the onlookers did not cry out their praises, the stones of that rocky land would have shouted out instead!

He was a sorrowful king, for he knew the fate of the people who "did not recognize the time of God's coming" to them. But he was also bold. His language was forceful as he drove out those who made the house of prayer a den of thieves. Every day he taught fearlessly at the temple, knowing his life was safe in the timetable of God's will.

My Response

Memory Point

On a 3x5 card, copy a new Key Verse: "Heaven and earth will pass away, but my words will never pass away" (Luke 21:33). Place the card where you will see it often and begin memorizing this verse.

☐ PRAY to apply God's Word

O God, help me to recognize the times of your personal coming to me in love . . .

61

☐ **PRAY for insight into God's Word**

Help me, Holy Spirit, to take in and to understand the teaching Jesus gave during his last days in Jerusalem.

☐ **READ Luke 20:1–19**

☐ **MEDITATE on God's Word**

Discovery

1. The chief priests and teachers of the law were upset by Jesus' actions in 19:45 and 47. What possible answer could Jesus have given to their loaded question in verse 2? How did he avoid their trap?

2. Interpret Jesus' parable: Who owns the vineyard? Who are the ones the servants treat wrongfully (10–12)? How do the tenants react to the son? What does the owner of the vineyard decide to do? Who are the "others" (16)?

3. Jesus quotes Psalm 118:22. Who is the stone the builders rejected? How crucial is this stone?

4. How did this parable answer the question of "authority" for the Jewish leaders? Does it answer the question of authority for you?

Reflection

In presenting the truth, Jesus used reason, parable, and Scripture.

Reasoned argument (1–8). The hostile priests and scribes were "trying to kill him" (19:47–48), but Jesus replied to their question by confronting them with another one. Whether they gave a positive or negative reply to his question about John's ministry, they would be self-condemned. To assert that John's ministry was from God would expose their disobedience; to say it was not would infuriate the people. We need to use our *minds* as Jesus did in "preaching the gospel" (1).

An unforgettable story (9–16). Jesus predicted his own death (13–15) at the hands of the religious leaders, the unworthy tenants of God's vineyard. He also warned again that those who do not use God's gifts responsibly will have them taken away and given to others. The listeners were horrified that other tenants might be given the Lord's vineyard (16)—even Gentiles (Acts 13:46–48).

Relevant Scripture (17–18). Jesus used Old Testament Scripture effectively against the Devil (4:1–12), with his opponents (20:17, 41–44), and for his friends (22:37).

My Response

Memory Point

Take your 3x5 card with Key Verse 5 (Luke 21:33) and place it on the mirror. Say the verse aloud several times today.

☐ PRAY to apply God's Word

"The stone the builders rejected has become the capstone; the LORD has done this, and it is marvelous in our eyes. This is the day the Lord has made; let us rejoice and be glad in it" (Psalm 118:22–24). Lord, help me to rejoice that you have sent the Son, whom you love (Luke 20:13), for my sake . . .

62

☐ **PRAY for insight into God's Word**
Lord, help me to show integrity and straight thinking in my opinions and actions, that I may reflect the grace of your character.

☐ **READ Luke 20:20-40**

☐ **MEDITATE on God's Word**

Discovery
1. How did the religious leaders hope to trap Jesus? What did they pretend?

2. What observations can you make about the way Jesus unmasked their loaded political question? Is Jesus' answer (25b) a good principle for living? Why?

3. What was inconsistent about the questions the Sadducees asked Jesus? What point were they trying to make?

4. How did Jesus answer their *real* question about the validity of the resurrection (37-38)? What does it mean to you that God is the God of the living, and not of the dead?

Reflection

Christ's opponents asked him two trick questions—one concerning this life and the other about the life to come.

Taxes (21–26). Obviously the taxes imposed by the Roman authorities were exceedingly unpopular. During Jesus' childhood there had been a Galilean rebellion over taxation, and he was certainly aware of the intentionally provocative nature of the question. If he said the tribute was to be paid, he would appear to be pro-Roman; if not, he could be reported as a subversive opponent of Rome. Jesus insisted that it was not "either/or" but "both/and." They must meet God's demands *and* Caesar's. By a clever reference to the coin's image, he asserted that, bearing Caesar's superscription, it must be given back to him as proper payment for the government services the people had received (Rom. 13:7). But man also bears God's image (Gen. 1:27), so he must also give himself back to the One who created him.

Resurrection (27–40). The Sadducees posed the ridiculous question of the woman with seven departed husbands in an attempt to present the idea of a physical resurrection as an absurdity. Jesus pointed out that the next life is a totally new existence, not a mere repetition of this one.

My Response

Memory Point

Review Key Verse 5 (Luke 21:33) and consider how this verse underscores Jesus' authority.

☐ PRAY to apply God's Word

Thank you that you are the God of the living, dear Father, and that you promise eternal life to all who trust in you. Thank you that you are my Lord and my God . . .

63

☐ **PRAY for insight into God's Word**

Lord, you have so much to teach me about honesty and openness in communicating with others. Help me to speak and to listen as one of your children.

☐ **READ Luke 20:41–21:4**

☐ **MEDITATE on God's Word**

Discovery

1. What did Jesus want the religious leaders to understand about who Christ is?

2. Of what did Jesus accuse the teachers of the law? Express the answers in your own words.

3. In contrast to the teachers of the law, how did the widow encourage Jesus? What was her attitude before God?

4. What principle of giving do you find in Jesus' response to the widow's gift?

Reflection

Now Jesus puts a question to his opponents regarding the Messiah. The rabbis all taught that Messiah was David's son, but Jesus says he is far more than that. Psalm 110 itself states clearly that David referred to the Messiah as his "Lord." Therefore Jesus insists that, though he is David's son, he is far more. He is the awaited Lord, God's only son.

The avaricious and pretentious scribes (46–47) were greedy for gain, but the poverty-stricken woman was commendably generous. She gave everything to God. Their ostentation and pride sharply contrasts with her humility and trust in God. At the end of the day they returned to their rich houses and lavish meals, but she went home empty, relying only on God. Luke's gospel shows special interest in the poor (4:18; 7:12–17, 22; 14:13, 21; 16:20; 18:35).

This passage has a lot to say to us about humility (45–47) and sacrificial generosity. Christians must be meek, for God resists the proud (1 Pet. 5:5–6). They must also be generous, as God is to us, in his astonishing, untiring grace.

My Response

Memory Point

Can you say Key Verse 5 (Luke 21:33) from memory? Try to repeat it twice, checking yourself to make sure you have it right.

☐ PRAY to apply God's Word

Grant me the ability to trust you, Lord, for the filling of my needs. Make me both fearless and wise in giving . . .

64

☐ **PRAY for insight into God's Word**

Heavenly Father, thank you for yourself, your reliability and constancy. I praise you that in a changing world you remain changeless and faithful. Help me to trust you more.

☐ **READ Luke 21:5–19**

☐ **MEDITATE on God's Word**

Discovery

1. What basic instructions did Jesus give to his disciples in these verses (8–9, 14, 19)?

2. Notice that these exhortations are Jesus' answer to the disciples' question of verse 7. What does that tell us about people who try to set dates about the end of the world?

3. What future happenings *did* Jesus predict in this passage?

4. In what way are the basic exhortations all that we really need to know as we face an uncertain future?

Reflection
In these verses Jesus taught much about the future.

Do not be deceived (5–8). Many first-century Jews believed that the temple was a sure sign of continuing stability and of God's presence in the midst of his people. Jesus exposed the futility of such misplaced confidence and warned his contemporaries of the temple's impending destruction. They must not trust in external things, but in God alone. Jesus told them, however, that the collapse of the temple would not usher in the end of the world. False prophets and messianic pretenders would arise in every generation. Christians are not to be misled by such deceptive messengers (1 John 4:1–6).

Do not be afraid (9–12). Jesus knew that the days ahead would be difficult for his followers. He did not promise believers an easy time. The end-events would be ushered in by fierce international strife, cosmic disturbances, and economic deprivation. But prior to that, in every generation Christian witness would be set within the context of physical harassment, rejection, persecution, arrest, and imprisonment.

Do not be silent (13–19). Such humanly daunting circumstances are opportunities to testify (13) and to trust (18–19). When we need them, he will give us words to say (14–15) and the strength to say them.

My Response

Memory Point
Review Key Verse 5 (Luke 21:33) and consider the trustworthiness of Jesus and his Word.

☐ PRAY to apply God's Word
Pray for those in far places who are in prison today for following Christ, and for those whose parents disown them because of their faith. Ask God to write Jesus' exhortations on your own heart . . .

65

☐ **PRAY for insight into God's Word**
Lord, reading the newspaper fills my heart with fear for the world and all who live in it. Teach me from your Word what my attitude should be toward uncertainty.

☐ **READ Luke 21:20–38**

☐ **MEDITATE on God's Word**

Discovery
1. Jesus predicts two events: 1) the destruction of Jerusalem (20–24) which took place in A.D. 70, and 2) the signs of the end of the age (25–28). What instructions does he give for each event (21, 28)?

2. What will be the mood of people at the end of the age? What is the point of the parable of the fig tree?

Note: Verse 32 is confusing. "This generation" may mean those living in the end time who will see the last events begin and conclude; or it may refer to a race of people—specifically, the Jews.

3. Although the material universe is unstable, what does Jesus say is permanent?

4. What attitudes are important for disciples who face an uncertain future (34–36)?

Reflection

Here Jesus speaks about impending (32) and ultimate (27) events. The predicted destruction of Jerusalem (20–24), which took place in A.D. 70, provides a scenic backdrop for far more disastrous circumstances—not the capture of a city (24), but the shaking of the heavens (26). In such times believers are expected to be:

Alert (25–28). They take Christ's warnings seriously and look for the signs of his coming (which resemble the budding trees announcing the approaching summer).

Confident (27–28). Terrified by these events, unbelievers will faint with fear (26), but Christians will be neither bewildered nor despondent. For them it is not a time of distress and destruction, but of expectation and redemption.

Careful (34). Christ's teaching about the future is not meant to promote speculation, but to inspire holiness (Rom. 13:11–14; 1 Thess. 5:4–6; 1 John 3:2–3).

Prayerful (36). In difficult times true Christians will seek God for the strength to retain their stability.

My Response

Memory Point

Notice the context of Key Verse 5 (Luke 21:33) from the study today. Say the verse aloud five times.

☐ PRAY to apply God's Word

Thank you, God, for your faithfulness and trustworthiness. I pray that I will be able to "stand before the Son of Man" (36) unashamed when he comes for me . . .

6/Jesus' Last Hours with His Disciples
Luke 22:1–53

☐ Introduction

My sister drew a dark-red knitted sweater vest from the chest. "This was Dad's," she said. "I knitted it for him, and he loved wearing it. I can still picture him in his chair, wearing this sweater and reading the newspaper." She paused, obviously remembering, and then said, "I've kept it all this time to remember him by."

Our lives are full of keepsakes. "Aunt Sally gave me this." Or "This is my dad's fishing rod." Mementos remind us of certain people. Even our behavior is marked with memories. I do things a certain way because "my mother did it that way." It's a subconscious way of carrying on memories, lest we forget the people who have been important to us.

Jesus knew how easily human beings forget. His purpose for coming to earth was about to be fulfilled. Then he would be returning to his heavenly Father. His disciples—and those disciples who would live in generations yet to come—needed something tangible that would help them remember. At the Last Supper that Jesus ate with his disciples, he instituted a ceremony, a symbol, that would remind the disciples of himself, of his death, and of his coming again. "Do this," he said. "It will help you remember me."

The bread represents his broken body; the cup symbolizes his poured-out blood. "Do this," Jesus said, "until I come again!" It is a memorial service for disciples. We remember Jesus—his life, his death, and his promised return—when we take the bread and the cup at the Lord's table. Someday the need for memorials will be over, but until he comes again, we need to keep on remembering.

Yet a traitor sat at the table when Jesus first distributed bread and wine to his disciples. It's possible to have a place at the table, to hear Jesus speak, to go through remembrance ceremonies, and yet to be full of selfish ambition.

It's a serious business. That is why Paul gave such strong warnings in 1 Corinthians 11:27–32.

Jesus' Last Hours with His Disciples/Luke 22:1–53 **151**

☐ Key Verse 6: Luke 22:26–27b
The greatest among you should be like the youngest, and the one who rules like the one who serves . . . But I am among you as one who serves.

☐ Outline of the Gospel of Luke

I. Birth and Childhood Narratives   1:1–2:52
   A. John's birth and mission foretold   1:1–25
   B. Jesus' birth and mission foretold   1:26–56
   C. Zechariah's blessing   1:57–80
   D. Jesus' birth   2:1–40
   E. The boy Jesus at the temple   2:41–52

II. Preparation for the Good News   3:1–4:13
   A. John the Baptist's ministry   3:1–14
   B. Jesus' baptism   3:15–23
   C. Jesus' temptation   4:1–13

III. Jesus in Galilee   4:14–9:45
   A. Jesus in Nazareth and Capernaum   4:14–44
   B. Jesus' call to faith   5:1–6:11
   C. Jesus' call and teaching of the Twelve   6:12–49
   D. Jesus' compassion   7:1–50
   E. Understanding Jesus' ministry   8:1–56
   F. Understanding who Jesus is   9:1–45

IV. Traveling toward Jerusalem   9:46–19:27
   A. Realities of discipleship   9:46–10:42
   B. Teaching about prayer   11:1–13
   C. Jesus' response to criticism   11:14–12:12
   D. Jesus' instructions to his disciples   12:13–12:59
   E. Call to repentance and faith   13:1–35
   F. Teaching about values   14:1–16:31
   G. Forgiveness and faith   17:1–19
   H. The coming kingdom   17:20–18:30
   I. Jesus nearing Jerusalem   18:31–19:27

V. Jesus in Jerusalem   19:28–21:38
   A. Triumphal entry   19:28–48
   B. Teaching in the temple area   20:1–21:4
   C. Signs of the end of the age   21:5–38

VI. Jesus' Last Hours with His Disciples   22:1–53
   A. The upper room   22:1–38
   B. In the garden   22:39–53

VII. Arrest and Crucifixion   22:54–23:56
   A. Denial and mockery   22:54–71
   B. Trial   23:1–25
   C. Crucifixion and burial   23:26–56

VIII. Resurrection   24:1–53
   A. Empty tomb   24:1–12
   B. Road to Emmaus   24:13–35
   C. Joyful disciples   24:36–53

66

☐ **PRAY for insight into God's Word**
Lord, help me to see beyond the details of events in today's reading—to see your incredible grace in human history.

☐ **READ Luke 22:1-13**

☐ **MEDITATE on God's Word**

Discovery
1. What problems did the chief priests and scribes face in dealing with Jesus?

2. How did Judas's treachery aid their cause? How do you account for Judas's actions?

3. Who was chosen to finalize preparations for the disciples to eat the Passover feast together? What preparations had Jesus evidently already made? Why do you think there was such secrecy about the location?

4. Who was in control of the timing of Jesus' arrest? What evidence do you see of our Lord acting sovereignly in this passage?

Reflection

What a poignant moment in the life of Jesus Christ! The right time had come. He knew what the future held. Verse 7 gives us both the history and the symbolism of the event.

His opponents (1–2). Only one thing appears to have worried the religious leaders—Christ's immense popularity with the ordinary people of his day (22:2; 19:48; 21:38; Mark 12:37). In his invincible sovereignty God used this "fear of the people" to keep the chief priests from an earlier arrest. It was his plan that Christ should die at Passover time, when the unblemished sacrificial lambs were offered (1 Pet. 1:19).

His betrayer (3–6). Maybe Judas was disillusioned with Jesus; his "fee" hardly supports any motive of monetary gain. Some scholars suggest that Judas wanted to precipitate a crisis that would force Jesus to demonstrate his power. The Devil can use apparently worthy motives as well as obviously evil ones to forward his schemes.

His control. The New Testament insists on Jesus' foreknowledge of Judas' treachery (21–22; John 6:70–71). Hence the secrecy in verses 7–13 points to a previously made arrangement. Judas would be listening, and the Upper Room would be a convenient place for the betrayal. But Christ had so much to share with his disciples. So he took these precautions against interruptions there and chose both the time and place of his betrayal (39).

My Response

Memory Point

"The greatest among you should be like the youngest, and the one who rules like the one who serves . . . But I am among you as one who serves" (Luke 22:26–27b). Copy Key Verse 6 on a 3x5 card. Say it aloud five times. Then place the card where you can review it throughout the day.

☐ PRAY to apply God's Word

Lord Jesus, when I see your gracious actions in this passage—knowing what was lying before you—I feel such love for you. Give me a portion of your grace, I pray . . .

67

☐ **PRAY for insight into God's Word**
Lord Jesus, let me see you in all of your love and grace as I study today. Warm my heart with your love.

☐ **READ Luke 22:14–38**

☐ **MEDITATE on God's Word**

Discovery
1. How did Jesus use the Passover to tell his disciples about his approaching death (14–23)? Why do we reenact the Lord's Supper in our churches (19)?

2. What effect did Jesus' acknowledgement of his betrayal have on the group? Was Judas responsible for his actions (22)?

3. What did Jesus teach the disciples about true greatness? What reward would the disciples receive for faithfulness?

4. How did Jesus warn the disciples that their life of discipleship would be more difficult in the days ahead (31–38)?

Reflection

Celebrating the Passover with his disciples was an important event in Jesus' life. This would be his last unhurried time with them, and he had many things to say to them. Given their level of understanding, imagine all of Jesus' emotions as he tried to give them a realistic idea of what was happening.

His predicted death (14–23). Jesus used the Passover as the occasion to tell his disciples again about his approaching death (19). It had all been determined by God (22). Although the prospect of such anguish was terrible, he still led his disciples in prayers of thanksgiving (17, 19). He knew that mankind was about to witness a great exodus—the redemption of the world, the end of sin's tyranny and slavery, through the sacrifice of the Passover Lamb of God.

His lowly example (24–27). The disciples quarreled about who ought to be regarded as the leading disciple (24). Jesus reminded them that pagans worry about such trivial things (25); believers should be eager to serve others, not rule them (27; John 13:4–5).

His prayerful love (28–38). Although Jesus must have been disappointed at their lack of love and pride (24), he recognized the kind, supportive things his disciples had done in the past (28), and he loved them. Their love for Christ and his kingdom ultimately would be rewarded. Jesus told his disciples that Satan had planned to ruin them *all* ("you" in verse 31 is plural), but Christ had prayed especially for *Peter* (32). He loves us as individuals despite our weakness and arrogance (see Matt. 26:33). His love for them was expressed in his prayers to God (32) and in his warnings to them (35–38).

My Response

Memory Point

Repeat Key Verse 6 (Luke 22:26–27b) from your 3x5 card several times so that you can begin to say it from memory.

☐ PRAY to apply God's Word

Lord, forgive me when I boast in myself instead of obeying the rules of the kingdom of God. Help me to have a servant's heart . . .

68

☐ **PRAY for insight into God's Word**
Dear Father, make my heart sensitive to you today, for my good and for your glory.

☐ **READ Luke 22:39–53**

☐ **MEDITATE on God's Word**

Discovery
1. What was Jesus' warning to his disciples in view of what lay ahead of them? In what ways is his warning appropriate for you?

2. What observations do you make about Jesus' prayer in the garden? What was his request? His struggle? His strength?

3. Why did Judas arrange for this kind of an arrest? Why did the chief priests consent to come for him in the dead of night, as Jesus himself queried (53)? See also Luke 19:47–48.

4. Describe how our Lord showed poise and graciousness in this difficult hour.

Reflection

Luke's account of Jesus' time with the disciples in the Upper Room and the Mount of Olives is brief. For more detail you will want to read John 14–16. Notice the assurance with which Jesus moves through these last hours before his arrest, and do not under-estimate how difficult it was for him.

His surrender to God (39–46). Jesus knew a secluded place at the foot of the Mount of Olives where he had often spent time with God (39–40). At no other time in human history was prayer more necessary, more costly, and more rewarding. It was *necessary* because Christ knew that he would soon battle the sinister powers of evil (Col. 2:15; Heb. 2:14; John 12:31). Christ looked to God for resources of strength and endurance, and was not disappointed. It was *costly* prayer. In his agony, the pain and desolation expressed itself physically (44) as well as spiritually. But the more the anguish increased, the more earnestly he prayed. It was *rewarded* prayer, not in that he was relieved of his agonizing task, but in that he was strengthened (43) to face it resolutely and endure it calmly. *Christ's primary concern in prayer was to discern and obey the revealed will of his sovereign, loving Father* (42). In our Christian life nothing is more important than that.

His compassion for people (47–53). Confronted by a traitor and surrounded by enemies (47–48), he performed the last miracle of his earthly ministry and healed the painful wounds of one of those who had come to arrest him. He will heal and restore his enemies if only they will look and believe.

My Response

Memory Point

Make certain you know Key Verse 6 (Luke 22:26–27b) because you will be learning a new one in the next study. Take whatever steps are necessary to put this key teaching of the kingdom of God firmly in your heart.

☐ PRAY to apply God's Word

Lord, my prayer life needs help. I'm either in too much of a hurry or I fall asleep as the disciples did. Give me a fresh sense of the importance of communicating with the living God . . .

7/The Arrest and Crucifixion
Luke 22:54—23:56

□ **Introduction**

What do you do in the face of terror? Suppose that telephone call comes in the middle of the night—the call that you imagined in your worst dreams, and now it is real: a life snatched away suddenly; someone you love hanging between life and death in the intensive care unit of some hospital; a fortune lost; an engagement broken; an unjust dimissal; a false accusation. How do we respond in the face of incredible stress?

Our response is inevitably linked to our attitude toward God. Some people are blind and deaf to God. He is irrelevant to them. They have chosen long ago to shut their ears and eyes to him. In the face of trouble, *they* are their only resource.

Others, who are sincere believers, may forget God for the moment. In the face of trouble they become utterly confused and incapable of coping. Their only thought is the present panic and how to get out of it. Only later do they remember the God who promised never to forsake them.

Those who know God well remember him in times of trouble as well as in joy. Their first thoughts go to him. He is in charge. Nothing takes God by surprise. The resource and power to cope is strong and sure: it is God himself.

You will see these human reactions in the characters who participate in the drama of the arrest and death of Jesus. The Jewish leaders are blind and deaf to God. They are bent on getting Jesus crucified, not listening to a message from God. Peter and the other disciples temporarily forget God in their terror. The situation seems out of God's control. It takes them awhile to remember.

In a class all by himself, Jesus remembers God. His serenity and certainty in the face of death is amazing. Don't forget that he was also a human being. But he knew his Father, and he knew who was in control.

A. W. Tozer, well-known author of a generation ago, said that the most important thing about a person was what he believed about God. It is this that determines his actions and his choices.

The Arrest and Crucifixion/Luke 22:54–23:56 **159**

☐ Key Verse 7: Luke 22:69
But from now on, the Son of Man will be seated at the right hand of the mighty God.

☐ Outline of the Gospel of Luke

I. Birth and Childhood Narratives *1:1–2:52*
  A. John's birth and mission foretold *1:1–25*
  B. Jesus' birth and mission foretold *1:26–56*
  C. Zechariah's blessing *1:57–80*
  D. Jesus' birth *2:1–40*
  E. The boy Jesus at the temple *2:41–52*

II. Preparation for the Good News *3:1–4:13*
  A. John the Baptist's ministry *3:1–14*
  B. Jesus' baptism *3:15–23*
  C. Jesus' temptation *4:1–13*

III. Jesus in Galilee *4:14–9:45*
  A. Jesus in Nazareth and Capernaum *4:14–44*
  B. Jesus' call to faith *5:1–6:11*
  C. Jesus' call and teaching of the Twelve *6:12–49*
  D. Jesus' compassion *7:1–50*
  E. Understanding Jesus' ministry *8:1–56*
  F. Understanding who Jesus is *9:1–45*

IV. Traveling toward Jerusalem *9:46–19:27*
  A. Realities of discipleship *9:46–10:42*
  B. Teaching about prayer *11:1–13*
  C. Jesus' response to criticism *11:14–12:12*
  D. Jesus' instructions to his disciples *12:13–12:59*
  E. Call to repentance and faith *13:1–35*
  F. Teaching about values *14:1–16:31*
  G. Forgiveness and faith *17:1–19*
  H. The coming kingdom *17:20–18:30*
  I. Jesus nearing Jerusalem *18:31–19:27*

V. Jesus in Jerusalem *19:28–21:38*
  A. Triumphal entry *19:28–48*
  B. Teaching in the temple area *20:1–21:4*
  C. Signs of the end of the age *21:5–38*

VI. Jesus' Last Hours with His Disciples *22:1–53*
  A. The upper room *22:1–38*
  B. In the garden *22:39–53*

VII. Arrest and Crucifixion *22:54–23:56*
  A. Denial and mockery *22:54–71*
  B. Trial *23:1–25*
  C. Crucifixion and burial *23:26–56*

VIII. Resurrection *24:1–53*
  A. Empty tomb *24:1–12*
  B. Road to Emmaus *24:13–35*
  C. Joyful disciples *24:36–53*

69

☐ PRAY for insight into God's Word
Lord Jesus, help me remember that you know what it is like to be lonely and to feel deserted. Encourage my heart today with your fellowship.

☐ READ Luke 22:54–71

☐ MEDITATE on God's Word

Discovery
1. What emotions and attitudes contributed to Peter's downfall? In what situations are you tempted to deny that you know Jesus?

2. What are your emotions as you read verse 61? Have you ever felt Peter's remorse? Compare Peter's response (62) with Jesus' words to him in 22:32.

3. What observations do you make about humankind from verses 63–65? What would have been the guards' attitude if they had known who Jesus was (69)?

4. Why was Jesus condemned by the council of the elders (66–71)? (See also Mark 14:63–64.) Look up and ponder the word *blasphemy* in the dictionary.

Reflection

Luke contrasts the weakness of Peter with the resolution of Jesus when confronted by sustained opposition.

Cowardice (54–62). Apparently Peter forgot the promise of Christ's resurrection and victory (18:33). Temporarily he lost his sense of eternal values and told lies in order to save himself from further questioning, mockery, and even arrest. How changeable we all are. We shouldn't be too hasty to accuse Peter of weak and unworthy conduct, for we too may have found it easier to make loud assertions of loyalty in congenial company than to speak a word of testimony to an unsympathetic crowd.

Courage (63–71). Jesus was exposed not simply to verbal questioning like Peter, but to physical assault and bitter mockery. When dawn came (66) they brought Christ before a hostile religious council, angered by his claim of equality with God. The clear biblical truth of Christ's deity is still regarded by many unbelievers as a totally unacceptable aspect of Christian doctrine. To refuse to acknowledge his unique Sonship is to dishonor his Father (John 5:23) and spurn his eternal salvation (1 John 4:15; 5:10–12).

My Response

Memory Point

"But from now on, the Son of Man will be seated at the right hand of the mighty God" (Luke 22:69). Copy this Key Verse on a 3x5 card and say it aloud five times.

☐ PRAY to apply God's Word

Father God, keep me not only from pride, but also from the sin of protecting myself with lies, as if you were not powerful enough to help me. Give me an honest, humble heart . . .

70

☐ **PRAY for insight into God's Word**
Lord, help me understand in a new way what the events in today's study meant to you; and help me remember that you stood condemned in my place.

☐ **READ Luke 23:1–25**

☐ **MEDITATE on God's Word**

Discovery
1. In contrast to Luke 22:70, of what did the assembly accuse Jesus in front of Pilate? What was their strategy?

Note: The Jews in the time of Jesus did not have the power to carry out a death sentence. Such an edict had to come from a Roman official.

2. How did Pilate try to avoid passing sentence on Jesus? Why did he finally give in to the mob?

3. Why did Jesus have nothing to say to Herod? (See Mark 6:17–20.) What indignities to Jesus did Herod permit?

4. What happened to people who refused to take Jesus seriously in today's study? What is the consequence of rejecting Jesus in today's world?

Reflection

In the story of Christ's last hours on earth we find ourselves in the company of weak men. There was Judas, either obsessed with the lust for money or disappointed with Christ's spiritual, rather than political, mission to his people. Peter was more concerned about his safety than his integrity. Pilate was evasive, ready to shift the responsibility on to someone else (5–7). Herod, utterly lacking in dignity and integrity, treated Christ with contempt simply because other people expected him to (10–11).

The Roman governor quickly discerned that Jesus was no fanatical zealot (4) and certainly not deserving of death (14–15, 22). He thought that perhaps it would satisfy the people if he whipped Jesus publicly (for what crime?) and let him go (16, 22).

The irony of these familiar events is both poignant and eloquent. Two enemies are reconciled (12). The serene peacemaker takes the place of the militant and disruptive insurrectionist; the life-giving Savior is deliberately rejected in favor of the man-hating murderer (25).

In the end, Pilate is swayed by the crowd, which was much the same sin as Peter's but on a much bigger scale. How sad it is when we allow ourselves to be carried along by the unthinking or unspiritual majority!

My Response

Memory Point

Try to memorize Key Verse 7 (Luke 22:69) by reading the verse twice and then reciting it from memory three times.

☐ PRAY to apply God's Word

Lord, make me strong in my commitment to you. Help me to be firm in the face of opposition . . .

71

☐ **PRAY for insight into God's Word**

Lord Jesus, you died in my place. Don't let this story ever become commonplace, no matter how often I hear it. Help me to meditate today on your great love.

☐ **READ Luke 23:26–43**

☐ **MEDITATE on God's Word**

Discovery

1. List the various people who had contact with Jesus as he went to the cross and hung suspended there. How did each one act toward Jesus? What do you observe about Jesus' response to them?

2. Compare the two criminals crucified with Jesus as to their guilt, their bitterness, their response to Jesus, and Jesus' response to them.

3. Could Christ have saved himself, as one of the criminals suggested (37)? See Matthew 26:52–54. Why wouldn't he save himself?

4. Verse 34 is a picture of humankind's stupidity and God's continual grace. How did the soldiers miss the cosmic significance of what was taking place? What lesson lies in this for us?

The Arrest and Crucifixion/Luke 22:54–23:56

Reflection

Even in the darkest hours of his life Jesus continued to think of others.

The distressed women who wept by the roadside were warned of the bitter experiences ahead for some of them and for all of their children (28–29).

The rough soldiers who drove the nails into his hands and feet were on his heart as he prayed that God would forgive their sins (34). During his life Jesus not only taught a totally different way of life (Matt. 5:11–12, 38–39, 44) but practiced it.

One of the thieves who was crucified with him joined in the cry of the crowd that Jesus should demonstrate his unique power by saving himself (35, 37) and his fellow-sufferers (39). But because Jesus wanted to save others, he refused to save himself. In Christ's dying moments one of the thieves acknowledged God's justice, his own guilt (41a), and Christ's purity, innocence, power, kingship, and eternal destiny (42). Have you made such an open confession of your need of Christ as Savior and Lord?

My Response

Memory Point

Keep your 3x5 card with Key Verse 7 (Luke 22:69) in a place where you can review it often. Notice the contrast between Jesus' position in today's reading and in this verse.

☐ **PRAY to apply God's Word**

O Lord Jesus,
When we see Thee, as the victim
Bound to the accursed tree,
For our guilt and folly stricken,
All our judgment borne by Thee,
Lord, we own, with hearts adoring,
Thou hast loved us unto blood;
Glory, glory everlasting
Be to Thee, Thou Lamb of God.
James G. Deck

72

☐ **PRAY for insight into God's Word**
Lord Jesus, thank you for the love which held you to the cross. My love for you is so weak; deepen it, O Lord, I pray.

☐ **READ Luke 23:44–56**

☐ **MEDITATE on God's Word**

Discovery
1. What events stopped the mouths of all the bystanders?

2. What was the significance of the curtain in the temple being torn in two? What do you think the priests thought when they heard the sound of the tearing?

Note: Only the High Priest could draw aside the heavy curtain in the temple and enter the Holy of Holies, representing sinful people before a holy God. Now it was torn in two—and in an unusual way—from top to bottom. (See Mark 15:38.)

3. Read verse 46 and compare it with John 10:18. In what way was Jesus in control of his destiny? Notice the manner in which he spoke in verse 46.

4. What do you know about the Joseph of verse 50? Why was his action a sign of courageous love? (See also John 19:38–41.) How would you have acted in such a circumstance?

Reflection

The crowds are silenced. The very heavens went into mourning at the sight of the Creator of the universe hanging on a cross. Suddenly the jeers of the rude crowd ceased. People began to beat their breasts and retreat in silence.

The way is open. The priests serving in the temple heard a tearing sound. The thick, heavy curtain separating the people from the symbol of God's presence was torn in two. The writer to the Hebrews explains the symbolism of this drama. He tells us that Christ "entered the Most Holy Place once for all by his own blood, having obtained eternal redemption" (Heb. 9:12). The way to God is now open because of Jesus' perfect sacrifice.

He gives his life. Jesus was no martyr. He gave his life for humankind. Instead of the feeble sighs of death, he cried out with a loud voice, committed his spirit into the hands of the Father, and died. A centurion praised God and exclaimed what was probably on the minds of many others. Later, when the soldiers came, they were surprised that he was already dead (John 19:31-33).

Joseph takes the risk of love. He was a member of the Council, and also a secret believer who must have known great pain as he watched the intense malice and scheming of the Sanhedrin. Joseph asks for Jesus' body and puts it in his own tomb.

So ends a most signficant day in human history. How does the story affect you? Do you know that you are one of the people for whom Jesus died that day?

My Response

Memory Point

Recite Key Verse 7 (Luke 22:69) from memory. If you do not know it yet, practice saying it several times. Notice how it gives a larger meaning to the events in today's study.

☐ PRAY to apply God's Word

Father God, the way is open to come to you because of the death of our Lord Jesus Christ. I come before you in his blessed name with great thanksgiving . . .

8/The Resurrection
Luke 24:1-53

☐ Introduction

"It's too good to be true!" We are better at planning the scenarios of disaster and disappointment than we are at imagining the best and most miraculous of happenings. We are surprised by goodness. "I can't believe it," we say. That is, of course, why some people refuse to believe the gospel. It seems too good to be true.

That is what makes the story of the resurrection so credible. No one expected Jesus to rise from the dead, even though he said he would. Even an empty tomb—a startling reality—was too good to be true. First reports were not believed. Angels' words were discounted. Two disciples, hearing the news, headed for home, heavy-hearted and discouraged. The horror of all they had been through still overwhelmed them. The stories they heard were too good to be true. Things like that just didn't happen.

But it did happen. The women's report was not an idle tale. The tomb *was* empty. The living Jesus took a walk with the two confused disciples on their way home and told them what the Scripture said. Have you ever been so weighted down with your problems that you couldn't discern that the Lord was speaking to you? Then you can understand what happened to these disciples. It took awhile for all of them to discover it wasn't too good to be true.

Suddenly their heaviness exploded into joy. What an incredible ending for what had seemed the end of all hope. That's the way it is with Jesus. He not only brings life; he *is* life.

Luke began this story about Jesus in the temple, with Zechariah serving at the altar. He concludes the story in the temple with the disciples praising God continually. It is a story of Someone so good—he is true!

☐ Key Verse 8: Luke 24:46-47

This is what is written: The Christ will suffer and rise from the dead on the third day, and repentance and forgiveness of sins will be preached in his name to all nations, beginning at Jerusalem.

The Resurrection/Luke 24:1-53   **169**

☐ **Outline of the Gospel of Luke**

I. Birth and Childhood Narratives *1:1–2:52*
   A. John's birth and mission foretold   *1:1–25*
   B. Jesus' birth and mission foretold   *1:26–56*
   C. Zechariah's blessing   *1:57–80*
   D. Jesus' birth   *2:1–40*
   E. The boy Jesus at the temple   *2:41–52*

II. Preparation for the Good News *3:1–4:13*
   A. John the Baptist's ministry   *3:1–14*
   B. Jesus' baptism   *3:15–23*
   C. Jesus' temptation   *4:1–13*

III. Jesus in Galilee *4:14–9:45*
   A. Jesus in Nazareth and Capernaum   *4:14–44*
   B. Jesus' call to faith   *5:1–6:11*
   C. Jesus' call and teaching of the Twelve   *6:12–49*
   D. Jesus' compassion   *7:1–50*
   E. Understanding Jesus' ministry   *8:1–56*
   F. Understanding who Jesus is   *9:1–45*

IV. Traveling toward Jerusalem *9:46–19:27*
   A. Realities of discipleship   *9:46–10:42*
   B. Teaching about prayer   *11:1–13*
   C. Jesus' response to criticism   *11:14–12:12*
   D. Jesus' instructions to his disciples   *12:13–12:59*
   E. Call to repentance and faith   *13:1–35*
   F. Teaching about values   *14:1–16:31*
   G. Forgiveness and faith   *17:1–19*
   H. The coming kingdom   *17:20–18:30*
   I. Jesus nearing Jerusalem   *18:31–19:27*

V. Jesus in Jerusalem *19:28–21:38*
   A. Triumphal entry   *19:28–48*
   B. Teaching in the temple area   *20:1–21:4*
   C. Signs of the end of the age   *21:5–38*

VI. Jesus' Last Hours with His Disciples *22:1–53*
   A. The upper room   *22:1–38*
   B. In the garden   *22:39–53*

VII. Arrest and Crucifixion *22:54–23:56*
   A. Denial and mockery   *22:54–71*
   B. Trial   *23:1–25*
   C. Crucifixion and burial   *23:26–56*

VIII. Resurrection *24:1–53*
   A. Empty tomb *24:1–12*
   B. Road to Emmaus *24:13–35*
   C. Joyful disciples *24:36–53*

73

☐ **PRAY for insight into God's Word**

Bearing shame and scoffing rude, In my place condemned he stood.
Sealed my pardon with his blood; Hallelujah! What a Savior!

Philip Bliss

☐ **READ Luke 24:1-12**

☐ **MEDITATE on God's Word**

Discovery

1. What did the women expect to find when they visited the tomb? Imagine the range of their emotions.

2. What three things surprised them?

3. In what ways did the angels exhort the women? (See also Acts 2:24.)

4. Why do you think the disciples were slow to believe that Jesus was alive? Do you ever miss what God is telling you because of your own different expectations?

Reflection

Those women who stayed near the cross saw where Joseph put the body of Jesus. It must have been a great encouragement to them to see Joseph's courage and the love with which he treated their Lord's body. Now it was time for them to be courageous, too. As the first streaks of daylight came, they were on their way to the tomb to anoint the body of Jesus.

They went (1). In recording the details of Christ's redemptive work, the gospel writers did not forget the ministry of devoted, courageous women. These women were the first visitors to Christ's tomb. The frightened disciples did not go there at first—possibly they did not want to be recognized as Christ's followers. But the women were determined to minister to Christ's last needs, even though it might be dangerous.

They remembered (8). The "two men" reminded them of Jesus' promise (6–7) that although he would be crucified by sinful men, he would rise from the dead on the third day (9:22). Although Jesus made that statement repeatedly, his disciples had been unable to accept it. How easily we forget the great promises of God's Word, which can transform our outlook and determine our destiny!

They told (9). Good news of a risen Christ is not "for private circulation only." It must be declared to all. The women shared the word even though their message was regarded as fanciful "nonsense" and unbelievable (11).

My Response

Memory Point

"This is what is written: The Christ will suffer and rise from the dead on the third day, and repentance and forgiveness of sins will be preached in his name to all nations, beginning at Jerusalem" (Luke 24:46–47). Copy this Key Verse on a 3x5 card. Practice saying it, thinking through the elements of the gospel presented in it.

☐ PRAY to apply God's Word

Lord, make me as eager to share the Good News as those women who went to the tomb early in the morning. How glad I am that you are alive today to be my Savior . . .

74

☐ **PRAY for insight into God's Word**

Lord, help me as I study today to see behind obvious facts to the realities that apply to my life today.

☐ **READ Luke 24:13–35**

☐ **MEDITATE on God's Word**

Discovery

1. This had been quite a week for the two people of verse 13 who had gone to Jerusalem to celebrate the Passover. Quickly think back over their experiences beginning with the triumphal entry (19:28). What events had they probably witnessed, which they now talked about (14)?

2. Now, heavy-hearted and on the way home, of what things were these two *unaware* as they walked along? Name at least three.

3. Why did their hopes die (21) the very day that their hopes were realized (24)? How did Jesus enlighten them? What part of the Scriptures had they failed to understand (26)?

4. What is the difference between hearing about an empty tomb (24) and having an experience with the living Lord? Apply this to your own life. (See especially verse 35.)

Reflection

Sorrow blinds the eyes to truths more powerful than the sorrow. How often has Jesus walked with us, and we have been unaware of his presence? On the day of his trimphant resurrection Jesus is still concerned for two dispirited people who walk toward their home.

Jesus on the road (13–27). The travelers did not recognize Jesus on the road (16) and similarly they had not identified him in the Scriptures. They told their fellow-traveler about the past (19–20), about their shattered dreams for the future (21), and about the bewildering present (22–23). But Jesus reminded them of forgotten truths revealed centuries before in Holy Scripture (27), just as the angels had reminded the women at the tomb of the great, but unremembered, sayings of Jesus (6–7).

Jesus on the threshold (28–29). Earlier in the day he "came up and walked along with them" (15), deliberately accompanying his anxious friends in order to deepen their knowledge, enlarge their horizons, and rekindle their faith. But now he "acted as if he were going farther" (28). He never forces his company on anyone. In patient love he waits to be invited in (Rev. 3:20). By his Spirit he will reveal his truth to those who are eager to learn, but he will not thrust his way into the lives of men and women who prefer to ignore him.

Jesus at the table (30–35). As he handed the broken bread to them they may have noticed, for the first time, the pierced hands. In the moment of their astonished recognition, he vanished, his mission accomplished. Despite the late hour, they made the long journey back to Jerusalem. Like the women (9) they too had something to tell (35). Jesus graciously made himself known to his disciples. Notice the apparent private appearance to Peter (34).

My Response

Memory Point

Review Key Verse 8 (Luke 24:46–47) by reading it aloud three times. Then try three more times to say it from memory.

☐ PRAY to apply God's Word

O Lord Jesus, make my heart burn as I hear you speak to me through the Scriptures. Thank you that you are eager to enter my life and reveal yourself to me . . .

75

☐ **PRAY for insight into God's Word**

Jesus, come in your risen power to bless my life this day. Enlarge my understanding and willingness to obey.

☐ **READ Luke 24:36–53**

☐ **MEDITATE on God's Word**

Discovery

1. Why were the disciples so frightened (37) when at that very moment (35–36) they had been talking about the risen Jesus? What was Jesus teaching them with his surprising actions?

2. How did Jesus try to calm the disciples' fears? Make a list (36–43).

3. How did Jesus emphasize the authority of his Word—both spoken and written (44–46)? What is your own conviction about the Word of God?

4. How much do you think the disciples understood after the ascension (51–53) about the purpose of Jesus' death (47–49)? How much do you understand about your responsibility to fulfill Jesus' words?

Reflection

In this majestic conclusion to his gospel, Luke says that Jesus did three things for his disciples:

He convinced them (36–43). If they told others that Jesus was alive, doubtless they would be told that they had seen a mere apparition. The rumor was spreading that the body of Jesus had been stolen by his friends. His followers needed convincing proof that Christ was physically alive. So he talked to them (38), invited them to touch him (39), showed his wounds to them (40), and even ate a meal in front of them (42–43).

He taught them (44–49). He told them about *God's purpose for his Son,* as he reminded them of Old Testament predictions in law, prophecy, and psalmody about the promised Messiah (44–47). Also he told them of *God's purpose for humankind.* The promise of the Father (49) was the gift of the Spirit (Acts 1:4–5) to be given to all kinds of people, Gentiles as well as Jews, so that the Good News of repentance and forgiveness might be declared to the world (47).

He led them (50–53). He "led them out" to Bethany where he had often prayed and talked with them. Though physically "he left them" (51), they knew that he was their unfailing companion (Matt. 28:20). They were joyful at last.

My Response

Memory Point

Begin by repeating Key Verse 8 (Luke 24:46–47) from memory. Then review all of the Key Verses you have been memorizing from Luke. Notice how these form an outline of the major themes in Luke's gospel narrative. Don't leave the study of *Luke* without knowing them.

☐ **PRAY to apply God's Word**

Dear heavenly Father, what Good News the story of Jesus is! Thank you not only for the model of his life, but also for the purposefulness of his death for me. Help me to be involved in proclaiming "repentance and the forgiveness of sins" in my own "Jerusalem" and beyond . . .

Prayer Notebook

| date | request | date of answer |

date	request	date of answer

date	request	date of answer

date	request	date of answer

date	request	date of answer

date	request	date of answer

God Is Speaking to Me About . . .

date

date

Key Verses

The verses printed below are from the New International Version.

Use the space below to copy the Key Verse from another translation if you wish.

Key Verse 1: Luke 1:37
For nothing is impossible with God.

Key Verse 2: Luke 3:6
All mankind will see God's salvation.

Key Verse 3: Luke 5:31–32
It is not the healthy who need a doctor, but the sick. I have not come to call the righteous, but sinners to repentance.

Key Verse 4: Luke 14:27
And anyone who does not carry his cross and follow me cannot be my disciple.

Key Verse 5: Luke 21:33
Heaven and earth will pass away, but my words will never pass away.

Key Verse 6: Luke 22:26–27b
The greatest among you should be like the youngest, and the one who rules like the one who serves . . . But I am among you as one who serves.

Key Verse 7: Luke 22:69
But from now on, the Son of Man will be seated at the right hand of the mighty God.

Key Verse 8: Luke 24:46–47
This is what is written: The Christ will suffer and rise from the dead on the third day, and repentance and forgiveness of sins will be preached in his name to all nations, beginning at Jerusalem.